Rays of Truth

Rays of Truth

PERSONAL REFLECTIONS—COLLECTIVE WISDOM

**Corporate
Unplugged
Forum**

Published by: Corporate Unplugged Forum
Text, Cover, and Artwork Design by: Markus Lehto

For information about Corporate Unplugged Forum
and the Corporate Unplugged Podcast, visit

www.corporateunplugged.com

ISBN (Hardcover): 978-91-531-0630-2
ISBN (Paperback): 978-91-531-0631-9
ISBN (Digital): 979-83-238-7607-5

Reflections on **Rays of Truth**

Rays of Truth contains timeless wisdom. Its diverse and accomplished authors have learned much from their experiences in the world and from their conversations with each other over several years. The result is moving and deeply necessary.

—**Amy C Edmondson** Novartis Professor of Leadership, Harvard Business School; Author of 'Right Kind of Wrong: The Science of Failing Well'

Rays of Truth is one of those rare compilations of wisdom that can heal us. We all carry around questions about life, success, and our personal truth. Trying to find answers to these questions can feel very lonely. This book is a companion on this journey. Twenty-six powerful stories of people who have dared to explore, dig deep, dig deeper, and find their burning core. *Rays of Truth* is like sitting around a bonfire with these people. It is insightful, challenging, thought-provoking, and feels like coming home.

—**Marie Ringler** Member of the Ashoka Global Leadership Group

Through the human-ness and open-spirit of the Corporate Unplugged Forum—as embodied through this new book—I have learned to practice an ancient Chinese way: absorb more, learn more, speak less, speak truths. I am very grateful for this community and its *Rays of Truth*.

—**Richard Hsu**, Cultural Strategist, Pan-Asia Network

Rays of Truth weaves a genuine inspiring web of human wisdom while sharing personal heartfelt and brave stories about the search for the same. Maybe the true meaning is not in the answers but in the questions. The book is a meditation of letting go of the riverbank and moving into the river of life, as we don't know where we are heading but life does. It is a true gift to be part of the journey of our group to now see and read this book organically born from Dreamers who Do.

—**Ulf Stenerhag**, Founder of Wayout, Chairman of the Board and Founder at African Bureau of Music

Imagine a small group of humans who voluntarily dare to take moments off the wheel of production, slow down, reconnect with the density of meaning that surrounds all of us, and reflect on how this density has guided their lives. Then imagine more. Imagine that these humans take more time off to weave their souls together, share their stories to create a tapestry rich with learnings. Now, open your eyes. The fruit of your imagination is right here in your hands. *Rays of Truth* is a rare gift from humans to humans. It could not have been planned. It could only be imagined, and hoped for. Now, it is real.

—**Roberto Verganti**, Professor of Leadership and Innovation, Stockholm School of Economics; Author of 'Design Driven Innovation'

Rays of Truth is a warm reminder of what can happen when we tune into our inner voice and deeply listen. In a world where the space between natural and unnatural, authentic and inauthentic is becoming increasingly blurred, it provides valuable guidance for self-reflection and navigating the complexities of our time.

—**Emre Eczacıbaşı**, Board Member, Innovation & Entrepreneurship Coordinator, Eczacıbaşı Holding

The world needs dreamers and the world needs doers.

But above all, the world needs dreamers

who do.

—Sarah Ban Beathnach

Photo by Mini Gemoll *Capri 2021*

In 2020, I was inspired to bring together a beautiful group of people who share complementary values and dreams. People who I consider as a gift to this world—with sharp minds and good hearts, who choose wise action over clever words. Business leaders, entrepreneurs, investors, professors, philosophers, neuroscientists, creatives, artists and utopianists who embrace the impossible and typically ask: "How can I serve? What can I give? What more can I do to move the needle of change?"

Sensing deep into these questions over monthly meetings and annual retreats, we have blossomed into the *Corporate Unplugged Forum* community. This book has been co-authored by some of our most passionate members.

I trust that this book has come to you for a reason.

It is a hopeful journey into the minds and hearts of people who are dedicating themselves, their organisations, companies, networks, and resources to better society.

In essence, this book is a testament to the power of personal reflection and collective wisdom. Each essay responds to the core question: "*What do I know to be true right now, and how did I come to that realisation?*" It aims to uncover personal gems of wisdom that are not ours to keep. Our wish is to pass them on to you.

Hopefully our courage to share will produce a ripple that radiates goodness out to the world.

Vesna Lucca
Founder of Corporate Unplugged Forum

Corporate
Unplugged
Forum

The **Corporate Unplugged Forum** *is an invite only space for global leaders to explore ideas, learn, share, and design actions for a wiser future.*

We build our collective intelligence by openly sharing our diverse perspectives and expertise. We have a deep desire to evolve, to find more ways to serve, and to deeply connect with people on the same quest.

Who We Are

We are leaders with good hearts and sharp intellects. Connected as compassionate human beings driven to creatively explore the complexity of our era.

What We Want to See

- More dreamers who do.
- More people with the courage to care and act.
- Success, redefined in a way that is all about how much we contribute.
- A humane, inclusive and regenerative approach to all life.
- A collaborative, just, and peaceful civilisation that evolves in balance with nature.
- Cultures and organisations capable of inclusive and continuous learning in the face of complexity and constant change.
- A co-created new narrative, inspired by ancient wisdom, organic principles and the future we want to see.

Sensing the Path of the Unseen

As a community, we have reflected numerous times on the concept of growth. Also around how the Corporate Unplugged Forum can grow while keeping the magic. Some of the questions we have aligned around are: *How can we serve more and share what is precious with more people? What are the key components of a meaningful journey? Who is there? What is happening? How does it feel to be there?*

While our journey continues, we have sensed into a few truths that offer guidance along the way.

Scaling deeper

We have no intention to make the Forum capture the spotlight or grow for the sake of growth. There is a certain beauty that emerges from scaling through depth instead. It offers an open endedness that relieves tension and the growing pains we are used to. It is an organic, human system—an expression of togetherness without ambition, without the distortions that come with salesmanship. There is a freedom in not having such classic drivers present. It encourages other qualities to rise to the surface, like self motivation, and our own sense of aspiration, empathy and compassion. These can only emerge when you have no mission or specific agenda. Scaling deeper is actually about *becoming*, which is an act of love.

The Corporate Unplugged Forum is a place to experience this unplugged-*ness*, where we can trust one another without any expectations and really focus on the process that emerges.

Experiencing something that comes from going deeper, from peer sharing, and from losing 'self' as you are experiencing togetherness and interbeing with one another. That is the only point. And that kind of intimacy can only happen when there is no expectation of outward growth.

The Compass of Joy and Excitement

So, what is the next step for the Forum? I don't know. We don't know. We choose to trust joy and excitement for guidance. We are now in territory where there's no authority to set a standard of what's great or good enough. What we're doing is not *there*, there are no awards, no official recognition by authorities who have come before us. We are in new territory. We're not the only ones; but, it is a new territory. If you're in the ordinary business world, you get a promotion or an award that tells you 'yes, you've done well, you've done enough.' But, we've stepped out of that place now. Nobody is going to tell us we are doing well, so we have to source our guidance from somewhere else. And that comes from joy and excitement and the feeling of being alive. When you orient toward that, then the next thing will become very attractive to you and attracted to you.

We don't think that we have to force growth in order to have a bigger impact. We can naturally grow by following what feels alive, joyful, and in service to life. The whole idea of growth needs to be questioned. *What do you think?*

The Power of Group Mind

The idea of group mind is fascinating. The gathering of diverse minds, united by shared values and intentions, somehow creates a synergy that transcends our individual capacities. It is like an independent organism is created giving us the freedom to get out of our individual mindsets and see things with clarity from a whole perspective, raising our consciousness.

Walking the Invisible Path

Where we need to go most today are the places where you may not get rewarded or celebrated. Breaking new ground is hard. But, that's how real change starts. There is no map. It requires genuine leadership and a group of trusted people to get there.

Walking this path requires courage that comes from an ever deepening connection to our inner core. And from having a community of people who hold complementary values. So when the rest of society is not yet up to speed with the real value you are generating, you have a community around you that understands and supports.

Another beauty of being held in a group mind is that when you experience it—innovative, unexpected ideas and solutions emerge, coming from a depth that no single mind could achieve alone. Because when we are interconnected, there is this profound experience of shared humanity guiding us.

Evolving Together

We need each other, even just to recognise what we're doing. And to say "yeah, you're not crazy for doing this, this is important for the reasons that I see also." And then once you've established that friendship and trust, then you can also ask each other the hard questions that push the edges even farther. You grow together, you evolve together.

The Highest Form of Intelligence

Within the group mind of our Forum, we have experienced

so much *kindness*—which in many ways we see as the highest form of intelligence. It's not the same as being nice, or letting somebody have their way, or avoiding uncomfortable truths because they are awkward. The word 'kind' comes from the same place as *kin*, or *kin*dred, which means that we are inseparable, that we are in relation. Imagine kindness as a transformative force. By weaving kindness into the fabric of our interactions every day, we are contributing to a collective shift in consciousness that echoes far beyond our personal actions.

True Alignment

The more complex our world becomes, the more we can sense the need for our hearts, minds, and bodies to align. Only then can we witness *harmony* and know that the irrational call of our hearts is not so irrational after all. When we finally let ourselves be guided by our hearts, the way appears—showing us the new realities waiting to be actualised.

—

The story of mankind is in you,

the vast experience, the deep-rooted fears, anxieties,

sorrow, pleasure and all the beliefs that man

has accumulated throughout the millennia.

You are that book.

—**Krishnamurti**

Weaving **our Truths**

This collection of short essays are personal contemplations that encapsulate and celebrate the diverse perspectives, expertise, and experiences within our community of *Dreamers Who Do*.

Our courage to share comes from the powerful experiences of alignment, togetherness, and community we have developed over the years.

Each essay shares a piece of truth that the author has arrived at through their life journey so far. We hope that these stories may be helpful to you in your own search for a life well lived.

Our insights have emerged through a combination of experience, contemplation, and practice. Sometimes in sudden and painful ways. Sometimes gradually, as a deep knowing through the course of time. In all ways, they anchor us and guide us forward.

—

Adam Gazzaley is "grateful to have arrived at a framework through my science and experience that has led me to a deeper understanding of myself and my place in nature. It has given me structure to more firmly decide how I want to live and the person that I want to be." It is a task of utmost importance. "We need to level up our minds to effectively address the many crises that threaten our existence... We suffer because we have allowed ourselves to stagnate in a level of reception-expression that serves the self and immediate outcomes, but does not nurture relationships with others/nature, and thus fails to promote our long-term survival on this planet." He shows us how "we do not exist as an island of I, but a world of we—integrated elements of a vast, interconnected, dynamic network."

Now is the time to act. This is the truth that **Nichol Bradford** holds. "Whatever you want to learn, just do it. That's the best way to learn... Everyone is making it up as they go along. And you have less time than you plan. There's plenty of time, but no time to waste. Just do it." She reminds us that since "it's about the journey, how that journey feels is what matters most."

What then is truth? Is it even possible to know what is true, conditioned as we are by our own senses and preconditions? In **Jacob Notlöv**'s words "If the use of reason is just my biological neural network ticking away in my head, what remains?" To him, and to most of us in the Corporate Unplugged Forum, the answer is love and care. And we all believe that love and care are transformative when put into action.

Bob Chapman had this powerful insight after years in his global conglomerate and dedicated himself to becoming "a caring people-centric leader dedicated to stewarding the lives in my span of care." He moved on to transform the corporation and developed a caring leadership education curriculum that now reaches far beyond his own organization. His truth shows how business can be a strong force for good, when used intentionally.

To **Jason Lippert**, this is logical. Because "The real benefit of truly living out a genuine culture founded on good values that are followed and upheld consistently is that your people will be happier, healthier, more trusting of leadership, leading themselves better and leading others better."

To be a leader is to serve. After a long spiritual journey, **Eda Çarmıklı** returned to the board rooms of her family's company group with a giving approach that now propels positive change at a scale. "Paying It Forward is much more than a simple act; it embodies the universal law of cause and effect... When we embrace this approach towards life, we not only initiate acts of goodness but also set off a chain reaction of positive outcomes."

To **Rebecca Henderson** it is about asking the right questions. "How do we give substance to the idea that we are not only competitive, selfish beings, but also connected, cooperative, loving—and dare I say transcendent?" She continues, "what do we know about finding joy, when it will never be all right?" And "to realize that it's all about current experience and human relationships, not cognitive mastery?" What would teaching look like if these were our goals?

How do we arrive at truth, and recognise it as we encounter it? To **Charles O'Malley**, "Truth is much more closely related to not knowing—and searching for truth therefore is more to do with unlearning than learning." On his path, "journeying towards Truth is about giving up what we think we know and becoming open to not knowing." When we do this, "we can begin to listen to each other more genuinely, to meet each other more fully, and to discover wisdom in the most unexpected places. The Truth about the universe is that everything belongs here, everyone has a place here and, if we can get beneath the surface appearance, we see that every perspective carries some form of universal intelligence."

There is only one way to live our lives, walking our own path. But it may take a while to find it. We are, as **Neha Sangwan** puts it "each on a unique soul journey." She guides us through how to find it through the signals of our bodies. As coping strategies to early events, we deviate from "our own internal compass... when we achieve the world's definition of success, when it's not our own true calling, it often results in a feeling of emptiness." But when we turn inwards, "we may discover that every interaction, experience and conflict is an opportunity to grow and heal."

Big challenges and the pain arising from them, are sources for growth if accepted and listened to. **Karin Volo** healed from a near fatal illness and rediscovered the power of Gratitude. "There is a gift in both giving and receiving for each act of kindness... Seeing lives through the Lens of Gratitude reminds me that we are all humans having challenging life experiences but that we can always find things to be grateful for regardless of the circumstances."

Unhealed pain inside us has the potential to fuel transition to a new life, the transformation and creation of a lifework with deeper purpose. As for **Vesna Lucca**, a sense of loneliness that had haunted her since early years unexpectedly guided a bold exit from her successful life in the corporate world and the creation of the platform *Corporate Unplugged*. It holds a podcast show, a forum for global leaders, and a method for companies to evolve—contributing to the shift of the corporate world on multiple levels and influencing the lives of many.

Mia Bengtsson too, takes strength from her shadow aspects to embark on new adventures with purpose. "I realize more and more that to develop the muscles of the heart I need to stay and face situations where it is hard to love myself, where my ability to be patient and brave is challenged. And that is how I grow my soul." It is when we lift our gaze and see the whole perspective, our small part in the meaningful puzzle of life, that we can truly make a difference in the world.

How do you survive war? How do you find ground under your feet, when everyone and everything you hold dear are at threat. For **Liubov Shlapai**, courage lies at the heart of it, the courage to see yourself and the world as it is. To accept the situation, your own capacity and its limits, our responsibility to stay true. "Love allows us to perceive the world the way it is and still be present, even when it is nothing close to romantic." We cannot shy away from the cruelty outside and inside of ourselves, when we accept and clearly see the dark sides of existence, we will find a way to live through it and contribute with what we can.

Some challenges in life are daunting. How do we muster up the courage to face a threat as severe and existential as the climate crises? How do we take our part of the burden, contribute with whatever we can, without losing hope. Overwhelmed by her work within climate solutions, **Linda Lanzavecchia** "understood that climate change, and all other environmental issues, are simply symptoms of a greater dysfunction—the inability of humankind to protect our home and to live in a way that sustains future generations." As in any complex problem, no one can do everything, but everyone can do something. "What helped me most of all was my deliberate shift of attention to what I could influence; shifting from what is useful to what is meaningful... and live every single day with pure curiosity."

The biggest quest of all lies before us, creating a regenerative society in which all life thrives. Through her life work, **Lisen Schultz** has "come to realize that curiosity without care seems to result in cruelty. And care without curiosity is easily misdirected... we need guidance in our learning process, to develop respectful relationships with life." How do we develop into beings who understand and act from a place of truth? There are many paths but they all lead inside, to ourselves and our inner work.

When self inquiry has led us to a place of truth inside, the insight grows that our outer lives need to reflect that. It takes courage to change into the unknown, we need guidance to find our way.

Mario Solari found that we can seek help in "the stories and lives of those we admire most deeply, our heroes. Those individuals whose impact and influence on you has been profound and transformative... By examining the qualities in them that we admire, we gain insights into our own essence and what truly moves us. This process of reflection is not just an exercise in admiration but a deep, introspective journey into understanding the fibers of our own being."

Whenever faced with difficulties in life, **Jayce Pei Yu Lee** found solace in allowing creation to flow spontaneously from within, "recalling moments where I sat at my desk, pen and markers in hand, pouring my thoughts onto paper or on my iPad... The act of creating instilled within me a sense of courage, reinforcing my belief that I could overcome any challenges... Through steady writing, making and creating, I uncovered something true emanating from within, enabling me to witness, embrace who I am, and ultimately let go of the old self, moving onwards."

To **Laura Inserra**, music is the path: "music is one of the most powerful tools to experience the vibrational nature of existence." For her it is "a shelter... a way to calm down my inner and outer environment, a place where I rearrange chaos into order, create harmony and experience it with others... a way to transcend reality, evoke emotions, and describe the unseen world." To Laura, sound is such "a powerful metaphor to grasp the essence of the Universe."

Our inner work may well be to create contexts for others to grow. **Jan Broman** builds places where the power of art can transform us. "I have seen it so many times, how extraordinary art or music sparks something new inside a person. As if they suddenly realize an aspect of themselves they did not know they had. We cannot change people, but we can invite them to be more of themselves."

Those who had the fortune to experience a childhood connected to nature, belonging to a community lifted by strong values and creativity, know that this gift carries a responsibility. To pass it on to future generations, enhanced through one's life work and insights. **Markus Lehto** realized that he has drawn deeply from his heritage—which was filled with music and community—into every project and each environment he has created, relentlessly searching for ways to infuse their essence into a future that serves all. "There was no artificial hierarchy at any level... a sincere experience of interbeing that transcended generational gaps, species, thought silos, occupations and cultures... community is the magic created through 'common unity'... The real work of our life journey is to make more and more harmonious music, in all that we do, from the inside out, helping each other become better at it, and celebrating it. There is enormous power... in rich cultural exchange and real community."

Geetali Chhatwal Jonsson's journey weaves together the rich melodies of her Indian heritage with the evolving rhythms of life in Sweden. Appropriately, her name means 'the one who loves music'. Like the twenty-two notes of the classical Indian musical octave, her love for storytelling blossomed in a childhood filled with vibrant conversation and openness to the world. For her, the stories over the centuries are essentially the same, but we keep changing the context. "It is like the bard who sings at a moment in time to those who listen." Her writing is a path of self-discovery, peeling back layers to find an inner freedom that transcends rational thought—"the deeper I go the more I feel a sense of emptiness, like a portal to myself... I am surrounded by a sense of freedom." In this journey, she seeks harmony within herself and connection to the deeper resonance of human experience. Geetali says she feels "blessed that I am in a space of faith and knowing that all of us are on the same path".

So what is the meaning of life and how do we live in a way that honors the purpose we were born to serve? **Pia Rudengren** looks behind the curtains of every life to the very fabric of existence and how we are interconnected with the silver threads in a big tapestry. "We live in a world created by the collective mind and collective vibrations. Everyone contributes to the world we see around us. If we act out of self-interest, lacking compassion and integrity, we will create disharmony... Only that which is in harmony with the pulse of the heart at the center of the universe is real... To make a lasting difference we need to tune our own individual vibration... We cannot change what other people think or do, but we can change inside. We must become aware of and take full responsibility for the vibrations we are transmitting. Our feelings, thoughts and actions. Every single breath counts."

Raya Bidshahri's truth comes from a scientific approach, from astronomy. The awe we feel when looking up to the starry sky above and pondering our place in the universe, awakens in us the existential intelligence to contemplate life itself. "It reminds us that we are not just integral but precious components of the cosmos, with a profound responsibility to cherish and protect our tiny home in the universe... We are not merely inhabitants of the universe, but we are the universe in a human form... Our curiosity, our exploration, and our quest for knowledge are the ways through which the universe experiences and comprehends itself."

When we write the stories of our own life, we may access the wisdom and insights of generations before us through ancient stories and scriptures. **Ma Steinsvik** describes how they accompany our life quests, with meaningful guidance encoded within them. "When we try to live without the old stories, without contemplative practice... we become slow, frustrated and off-center. The external shift to a regenerative system must be accomplished through an internal shift... In an ever more challenging and complex world, we need to know how to move into inner stillness. There, we have the integrity to adhere to the value of all life, to the awe-inspiring heaven that is our Earth."

If we do cultivate our inner realms, if we have the courage to be dreamers who do, we can create a world of infinite beauty. **Raj Sisodia** reminds us that the "world is as you dream it. If you don't like the world as it is, you need to dream a better dream… Our life is the canvas on which we can deposit the outpourings of our soul to create something of lasting value and transcendent beauty." We have the gifts and capacity to "live in a way that at the end of our life, people experience deep grief, mingled with deep gratitude for the life we had lived and the lives we had touched."

Finally, **Rebecka Carlsson** emphasizes how important it is to formulate the insights and ideas we have nurtured into words and then share them with others. Humanity has the gift to communicate—coming from the word *communicare* which means "to make common, share or impart." When turned into speech, texts are given wings and spur the action of others. "To not give a speech when you have one to give is to not deliver someone else's Call to Adventure… It's actions that change the world, but words change our actions." Herein lies the purpose of this book: to—in a time of complexity and change—share the truth that resonates inside us. Because after all, as Rebecka writes, "what have people done in all times of crisis throughout history? They've come together in a circle and talked about it. So, now is a good time to convene—to listen to the world, each other, and ourselves—and talk about what's sacred and most important to us."

—

If Not Now, When?

We've been told the government has 'got it', technology has 'got it', science has 'got it'. But no. Now is the time for each and one of us to take responsibility and act. It is time for our collective intelligence—our connected minds and hearts—to bring our gifts to the table. It is time to weave our own Rays of Truth together.

We are all microcosms of the macrocosmos. Through our conscious choices we reflect principles of human nature that confirm 'here is what a human being does in the situation I was in'. We can be sure that the vibes we send out through our words and actions will be picked up by someone else, somewhere else. A deliberate act of kindness always inspires another one. We draw a lot of hope from that.

Our wish is to see humanity dedicated to healing itself, for us to heal each other and the Earth, motivated by a deep understanding that our planet is alive. Every ecosystem, every place, every forest, every river, every person is a sacred being that shares in this aliveness. To understand that 'their' health is our health, 'their' wellbeing is our wellbeing, inspires a sense of meaning, purpose, and unity. Now is the time to live what we are here for—the experience of a joyful life.

—

26 Authors
26 Personal Reflections
26 Rays of Truth

Adam Gazzaley

Cycles of Connection-From Reflex to Wisdom

Our species is desperately suffering. Despite extraordinary advances in science, technology, and medicine, humans ceaselessly harm each other and our natural world. Somehow, we seem uniquely unsuited to thrive in the very environment that we've created. We need to level up our minds to better live with one another and the rest of nature, as well as to effectively address the many crises that threaten our existence.

—

Breakthroughs can happen in the most unexpected of ways. For me, it was eight years ago, silently meditating in the presence of a majestic, old oak tree in the golden hills of Northern California. It was there that I experienced an expansion of my thinking that changed how I view myself in connection to the world around me. After 25 years as a neuroscientist, with countless hours spent peering through microscopes and analyzing neuroimaging data, it was startling to arrive at such a perspective-shifting insight about the mind, not via experiment, but by a transformative experience.

It was 2015, I had been invited to attend a 10-day Vipassana retreat by my dear friend, Jack Kornfield. Jack, a thought leader in the mindfulness field, was trained as both a Buddhist monk and clinical psychologist. He is also co-founder of Spirit Rock, the location of this silent meditation retreat. The truth is, I did not want to go. I was uncomfortable (even fearful) with the thought of being in silence and disconnected for so long. I also had no meditation experience at that time. But out of tremendous respect for my friend, and a genuine interest in the field, I agreed to attend.

Another challenge I faced, as I was preparing to leave for this extended time off grid, was putting the final touches on my book, *The Distracted Mind: Ancient Brains in a High-Tech World*. Although it seemed fitting to go on such a retreat after writing this book, attending to the details of submitting a final manuscript made breaking away difficult. However, in retrospect, I realize that it was the timing that engendered the breakthrough I experienced. You see, front and center in my thoughts was a deep concern about the fraught relationship we humans have with our environment. Notably, how destructively we engage with our technologies (a central theme of the book), but even more troubling to me was how egregiously we treat each other, the rest of nature, and our planet. The big question in my mind at the time was: Why?

I sat down on a floor cushion in the most elegant (yet simple), expansive (yet intimate), natural (yet intentional) chamber, perched on a hill in the woods. In every way, it was the perfect container for an extended inner journey. Surrounded by one hundred other voyagers, I began my first meditation session. I was instructed to focus on my breath, and when it wandered, to be aware of it and gently return attention to my breath without judgement. I quickly found that this was no easy task. In addition to being distracted by discomfort in my body, my mind kept drifting back to that big question. However, I took the charge seriously, and pushed myself to be present with my breath.

One approach that was suggested to help with meditating was to attend to the rhythm of breathing: inspiration > expiration > inspiration > expiration... This worked very well for me. I was able to quiet my busy thoughts and sink into the rhythm of my breath. But as the first two days slowly passed, the cyclical nature of respiration increasingly activated my thinking mind. I was struck, and not for the first time, by how rhythmic cycles are so fundamental and pervasive in nature. They exist externally (e.g. climate and lunar cycles) and internally (e.g. sleep-wake and menstrual cycles), and at astoundingly disparate timescales (e.g. Milankovitch cycles in our solar system occur once every 10,000-100,000 years, while gamma rhythms in our brain cycle 30-100 times every second). It is no exaggeration to view cyclical patterns as a fundamental aspect of the universe and all of life.

Most fascinating to me is the cyclical dance between the internal and external realms, from the large-scale exchange of elements between life and environment (biogeochemical cycles: e.g., carbon and nitrogen cycles), to vast ecosystems that emerge from the interaction of life and earth, fueled by nutrient and energy cycles (e.g., coral reefs and rainforests), to the powerful influences that abiotic factors exert on biological cycles (e.g., light and temperature modulate circadian rhythms). Breathing—my ever-present focal point—was a salient example of the criticality of these life-environment cycles. If the rhythmic exchange of elements between body and air halts for mere minutes, we die; this corporeal tether to the external world is so incredibly vital and fragile. With all this swirling around in my mind, it should be no surprise that I was once again struggling to focus on my breath.

The first insight rushed into my awareness at the end of the second day: Our failure to thrive in terms of our external interactions – the harm we inflict upon the planet (e.g. climate), other humans (e.g. war), and the rest of nature (e.g. biodiversity) —was somehow related to another fundamental cycle that connects life and environment, the perception-action cycle. This neuroscientific concept, coined by Joaquin Fuster three decades ago, describes the flow of sensory information into the brain from the environment to form perceptions, followed by actions that occur as a response, leading to changes in the environment that result in new perceptions, which in turn drive new actions, and on and on. This circular flow between reception (from outside in) and expression (from inside out) is the foundation of all animal behavior: perception > action > perception > action.

And so, this is where I found myself on day three, sitting in silence, trying to focus on my breath, with a nagging intuition that I had a clue to answer the big question in my mind, but was missing the 'aha' to pull it all together. I was also confronted with the very real struggle I was having with meditating. I just could not attend to my breath for very long, especially now that my imagination was stimulated.

Day four; I considered leaving the retreat. But a consultation with Jack impressed upon me the importance of pushing through this hurdle and getting over the midway hump, a time when many others were also struggling. He suggested that I try to find a way of meditating that worked better for me and encouraged me to leave the building and spend time outdoors during some of the sessions.

So, I took off alone, in silence, into the forested hills of Spirit Rock. It suited me well, being immersed in nature, smelling the foliage, hearing the birds, seeing the wind-blown patterns in the long golden grass, and feeling the warmth of the sun on my face. My frustrations evaporated, I felt calm and clear. I soon came upon the most glorious oak tree I had ever encountered and settled down on the ground in front of it. I decided to make this tree my meditation. It would be the sole focus of my attention, with my breath present as a silent companion and constant reminder of the elemental exchange between humans and trees.

This changed everything; I went on to spend many hours over the next two days deeply meditating for the first time in my life. It felt like I was adrift on a vast sea, gently rising and falling with the rhythm of my breath, yet firmly anchored to the Earth by the grounding presence of this ancient giant. Occasionally my mind wandered, but mostly I surrendered to perception without analysis, judgement, or decision. I experienced a unique sense of awareness-sans-thought embraced in those powerful branching arms, with sinewy roots bursting through the earth around me, moss-covered, wizened bark filling my gaze, and delicate branches gently beaming down on me with bright, green leaves.

It was day six, and I was over the hump. The passage of time became smoother, gentler, even routine. I was in flow; I had found my muse. And then after hours of focus it happened, when least expected, an experiential breakthrough. My perception of this magnificent tree evolved, first to a deeper sense of awareness than I thought I was capable of, and then beyond to a feeling I am inclined to call love, but that fails to capture the pure, unconditional, boundless, empathy and compassion I experienced. For the first time on the retreat, tears streamed down my face.

Over the remaining days, my mind felt like it was on fire as I experienced a connection with the same subject, at different levels, at the same time. I saw first-hand with increasing clarity that the perception-action cycle was just one level of a progressive hierarchy of reception-expression cycles. And that an answer to the big question might be found by better understanding these cycles. To be clear, I hold the concepts that define the perception-action cycle as foundational neuroscientific principles, and Fuster's scientific contributions to understanding its neural network basis in the highest regard. But this experience revealed to me the limitations in viewing this cycle as 'the' connection between brain and environment.

My perspective now is that a conceptual framework can be constructed around the perception-action cycle, with a more primitive cycle at its core and two higher levels of cyclical exchange between brain and environment accessible beyond it. To share this framework with you, and to capture a flavor of its experiential origins, I will present it through guided-imagery. Please attempt to generate in your mind's 'eye' the environment that I describe, and to feel in your mind's 'heart' the emotions that I convey.

Dance in the Meadow.

Imagine yourself lying on the grass in a glorious meadow just before sunrise. You are surrounded by beautiful wildflowers of every color, visible but still muted by the pre-dawn light. Turn your mind's eye toward the sky above you. Picture the gradient of color, from the warm glow of golden-red near the horizon, up into the heights where blue blends into indigo and then to pure black. Turn your mind's ear toward the meadow around you and hear the buzzing insects, but also notice the quiet and tranquility. Direct your attention to the varied smells: the fresh grass, sweet flowers, fragrant lavender. Feel the coolness pressing against the back of your legs and the palms of your hands as they rest upon the earth beneath you. Bathe in the totality of these sensations and be immersed in the meadow.

This is *perception*, a complex integration of information flowing into your brain from your sensory receptors. It is a construct, your personal interpretation of reality. It is represented in the back half of your brain, with each sensation having its own specialized area. But the signals merge to create a unified percept of you being in a place.

As the sun rises above the horizon, imagine standing and lifting your arms to stretch your body in the early morning light. Take a few steps towards the sunrise, and then stop and stand still. Inhale a deep breath of cool air, and slowly exhale.

This is *action*, a complex integration of movement commands from your motor system. It is represented in the front half of your brain. And although each movement occupies its own specialized territory, the signals merge together to generate cohesive and coherent actions.

Turn around so that you face away from the sun and notice the temperature drop on your skin. Walk slowly through the meadow, observing your long shadow gently dancing on the earth. Lightly swing your arms and feel the tall grass brush against your fingertips as you drift past. Notice that you have come upon a lavender bush; kneel and inhale deeply, smelling its rich, earthy scent.

This is the *perception-action cycle*, a continuous, rhythmic exchange between perception and action that connects you to the world around you. Your perceptions guide your actions, these actions in turn alter your perceptions, and round and round it goes. This is the basic function of your brain, to transform sensory input into motor output, and then back again to new input. This cycle between the environment and brain is the foundation of all animal *behavior*.

It becomes clear how fundamental this cycle is for life if we turn back the evolutionary clock and consider a more primitive version: the *sensation-movement cycle.* This cycle is central to how all organisms interact with the environment; it evolved for survival. It does not require higher-order brain functions needed for perception and action. It does not even require a brain or a nervous system. Even single-celled organisms, like bacteria, sense environmental stimuli such as nutrients or toxins, and either move toward or away from them. A young sunflower in the meadow senses the dawn light and steadily turns to follow it on its path throughout the day. All animals, including humans, retain sensation-movement cycles as part of their basic biology. These are known as *reflexes.* A sharp thorn leads to withdrawal of your hand, a bright light leads to constriction of your pupils. Automatic couplings between sensation and movement are still critical for our functioning and survival.

Appreciate how far interactions between life and environment have advanced as the brain evolved, from basic sensation-movement cycles to complex perception-action cycles. Although the latter can still present somewhat reflexively, i.e. actions without decision-making (i.e., habits), it is from this cycle that goal-directed behavior emerged throughout the animal kingdom. But humans engage in reception-expression cycles at a higher level than this one.

Taste the Berries.

Now picture yourself walking through the meadow and coming upon a bush full of succulent blueberries aglow in the midday light. Your perception-action cycle engages when you see these tasty berries and you reach to pluck them. But, please, pause before you eat the blueberries. Take a moment to appreciate the rich blue color and smell its tarty sweetness. Feel the smoothness of its skin between your fingertips. Now turn your focus inward to other perceptions that are present in your mind: Are you hungry? Are you curious? Are you excited? Are you bored?

This is *awareness*, a higher-level of perception that integrates externally-generated constructs with those in your internal milieu: thoughts, feelings, perspectives, biases, and judgements. The brain networks at play here are even more extensive. They involve connections between areas located on the sides of the front and back of your brain, guiding attention to the external world, and areas in the middle of your brain that enable introspection.

Go ahead and pop a blueberry into your mouth. As you go about eating it, turn your focus to the source of your actions in this moment: Do you really want to eat this blueberry? If so, do you want to slow down and savor it, or speed up and devour it?

This is *intention*, a higher-level of action that imbues behaviors with deeper meaning and purpose. There is, of course, still an influence of base urges, desires, yearnings, repulsions, and aversions, but actions in this cycle are guided by deliberate reasoning and decision-making.

Eat another blueberry with awareness heightening your perceptions and intentions guiding your actions. Notice the firmness of its skin on your tongue, the mix of sweetness and tartness that spreads across your palate, and the crunch of seeds between your teeth. But also, be mindful of the richer experience of awareness induced by your intentions to eat this berry, and your intentions to be aware of the ensuing perceptions from eating the berry. This higher-level cycle beyond perceiving and acting connects us in a deeper and more meaningful way to the environment.

This is the *awareness-intention cycle*. It is a far throw from the reflexive and habitual responses of lower-level cycles, spanning a spectrum from deliberate, goal-directed behaviors to *mindfulness* at its highest extents. From this cycle, constructs emerge of *self, mind, identity, and consciousness*. It is engagement in this higher-level reception-expression cycle that has enabled our species to accomplish remarkable feats of creating global societies, art, music, and technology.

There is a lot to celebrate here, but it is critical to recognize the significant cost incurred with the emergence of self and mind. It often manifests as a delusion that we are self-contained entities, perceiving with awareness and acting with intention, but as islands disconnected from others and the natural world—the island of *I*. This is the source of our desperate suffering. But fortunately, we humans have the potential to go higher still, beyond awareness and intention.

Embrace your Love.

Imagine yourself in this beautiful meadow at sunset, relaxing in post-blueberry bliss, when you see a love approaching—a spouse, a dear friend, a sibling, or a parent. When they get close, you see they are crying. You remember that their mother is sick, and you suspect that this is the source of their despair. Engage your awareness of their state. But now push beyond to discover that you are sad with them. Embody their grief as if it was your own. Sense the dissolution of the boundary between you.

This is *Empathy*.

Now reach beyond your intentions to comfort them and embody a deeper desire to relieve them of their suffering as if it was your own. Extend your care to them as an action and radiate your love.

This is *Compassion*.

Give them a tender, loving hug. Feel them in your arms, see tears flowing down their face. Notice how this highest-level of reception and expression naturally flows in a circular pattern: empathy > compassion > empathy > compassion. Also appreciate that the empathy-compassion cycle is not solely engaged for suffering, but for joy—and that it is not only achievable with other people, but with all of nature.

For thousands of years, societies around the world have recognized empathy and compassion as essential to cultivate for both personal and societal well-being. Notably, the brahmavihārā, rooted in ancient pre-Buddhist philosophies, taught of the central virtues of loving-kindness (mettā), compassion (karunā), empathetic joy (muditā), and equanimity (upekkhā) (fittingly, these are the names of the Spirit Rock residence halls; I spent nine silent nights in Karunā). Brahmavihārā, while integral to practices of Buddhism, Hindu, and Jainism, are regarded as universal and fundamental truths that extend beyond any specific religion, tradition, or culture.

The empathy-compassion cycle is a path to wisdom, a deep understanding that everything is truly connected; that we do not exist as an island of I, but a world of *we*—integrated elements of a vast, interconnected, dynamic network. With practice, the circular exchange of empathy and compassion between you and everything around you weaves an intimately interwoven tapestry of connection. This is what I experienced in the presence of that ancient oak tree after days of singular focus. This is why I was moved to tears.

—

Cycles of connection between reception and expression are a fundamental basis of being. Every life form engages in this circular flow between the internal and external. Humans have the privilege to access the full potential breadth of cyclical exchange, from sensation-movement (track the rising sun—the base of *reflex*), to perception-action (dance in the meadow—the land of *behavior*), to awareness-intention (taste the blueberries—the domain of self and *mind*), to empathy-compassion (embrace your love—the realm of *wisdom*). This framework of a progressive hierarchy of cycles of reception and expression serves as an instrument for us to better understand our connection to the world around us.

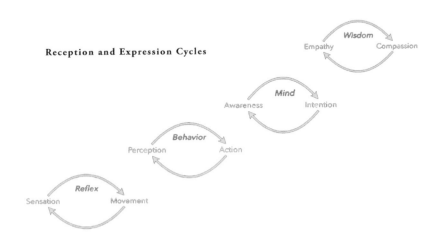

It has been 8 years since the Spirit Rock retreat. I have revisited the ideas born there in silence many times and in many ways. With this conceptual framework as a tool for enquiry, an answer emerges to the big question of why we treat each other, the rest of nature, and our planet so poorly: Because we allow ourselves to stagnate in levels of reception—expression that serve the self and immediate outcomes—but, do not foster meaningful and sustainable relationships with the external world, thus it will ultimately fail to support our long-term survival on this planet (i.e., perception-action and low-level awareness-intention cycles). Importantly, it also suggests that a path toward a healthier future with others and the natural world may be achieved by learning how to engage higher cycles of reception and expression (i.e., high-level awareness-intention and empathy-compassion cycles). One does not advance through cycles of connection like a student passing through grades of school. We continue to activate lower levels of reception-expression concurrently with higher levels. Reflexes and habits are ubiquitous in our daily lives, even for the most enlightened amongst us. But we do have agency to influence the composition of our interactions. Thoughtful and consistent engagement in certain experiences, like meditation and nature immersion, facilitate more frequent access to higher levels, which in turn fosters wisdom that potentiates the underlying cyclical process.

Spending more time, each passing day, in connections that activate the highest levels of awareness-intention and empathy-compassion is a route to a better existence on both a personal and universal level. We lead more meaningful and impactful lives by dissolving the delusion of separation between ourselves and the rest of nature, while simultaneously supporting our species' long-term survival by caring for our planet. There is a sort of cosmic harmony in this approach to alleviating collective suffering, in that these cycles of connection, the very fuel of our evolutionary journey from reflex to wisdom, are cousins to the vital, vast cyclical exchanges of matter and energy between life and environment that envelope the Earth.

This is a personal reflection. I am grateful to have arrived at a framework through my science and experience that has resulted in a deeper understanding of myself and my place in nature. It has given me structure to more firmly decide how I want to live and the person that I want to be. These perspectives have been invaluable, especially as we introduce our young daughters to a world that we share with millions of other species. I revel in our family discovering imaginative ways to unlock fresh perceptions, awareness, and empathy for trees that we meet on our wanderings —redwoods, sequoias, banyans, pines, willows, eucalyptus, elms, and, of course, oaks—and learning how to better engage with them through action, intention, and compassion. The benefits of these nature practices effortlessly extend themselves to all our other interactions.

This journey of discovery has been humbling. It takes time, effort, and patience to expand how we experience ourselves in connection with the rest of nature. I recognize that I do not spend as much time in the highest levels of reception-expression cycles as I wish I did. Working towards this objective will be a joyful pursuit for the rest of my life. My own limitations have motivated me to devote myself to developing and studying novel approaches to help others travel this path.

I dream of a future for my girls where empathy-compassion are as automatic for everyone as inspiration-expiration, present every day, and engaged for all of nature. Even shifting the currents slightly in the direction of this idealized vision, would be a meaningful step towards reducing our current state of desperate suffering. But such a shift does not take place via policies at the societal level, rather it must occur for each person, in their own way, and in their own time.

It is my sincere hope that your perceptions are bathed in loving awareness, that your actions are guided by kind intentions, and that you practice the dance of empathy and compassion, growing in wisdom each day. Humanity needs this, the earth needs this, all of nature needs this.

—

Adam Gazzaley *is a neuroscientist, neurologist, inventor, author, photographer, entrepreneur and investor. He is Founder & Executive Director of Neuroscape at UCSF and Co-Founder, Board Member, and Chief Science Advisor at Akili. He has discovered many diverse passions in life, each an opportunity to try to make this world a better place.*

Scan the code to access extra content Adam has created to support his essay such as AI visualizations and a recorded meditation.

Nicole Bradford

The Essence of Time: Lessons on Living Fully

Somewhere between life and death, love and heartbreak, the longing for and the missing of, you realize that ...

Lesson #1: *No matter how long you live, it's less than you planned.*

My teachers on this couldn't be more different.

One was an 83-year-old woman who defied any attempt to 'type her' as she racially integrated every school she went to from the 1950s onward. This woman was Carole Hill, my aunt, who was both my friend and my mother figure after my birth mother passed in my early twenties. I had just graduated from college and was about to take a job I didn't want, in a city I was done with, as a bridge to being ready to live. We were on the telephone, and in her typical gruff voice—likely with a cigarette and vodka tonic in hand—she said, "Nickki, if you lose your money, you can make more. If you lose your man, you can get another because there are so many of those. But, time... time you can never get back." And that's how she lived.

We snorkeled off the Great Barrier Reef in her 50s, enrolled in Tango School in Buenos Aires, Argentina in her 60s, and explored China, the Middle East, India, Africa, the Indian Ocean, Central America, South America, and the Caribbean together in her 70s (25+ countries). And I was lucky enough to be her person as her health shifted in her 80s. We spent the first half of 2023 fighting to keep her heart going and the second half saying goodbye before she passed just before Thanksgiving.

Even at the end, having lived so robustly, she wasn't done yet. In her last few days, she'd ask me to help her stand and I'd hold her up, bear her weight, so she could feel the ground under her feet and express her will, just a few more times before the end.

My other teacher was the 16-year-old son of a friend who was hit by a car while riding his bicycle to buy a snack. Before the accident, he was just about to launch—dating, looking at schools, rock climbing and more. He's a brilliant young man, who after spending three months in a coma, has staged a miracle of a comeback over the course of a year and is now able to climb stairs on his own! Still, his life has been changed in an instant. He was just going out for a bite.

Watching them both wrestle with life over 2023, one fighting the end of life and the other fighting for the beginning, branded this into me: Time is precious. None of us knows how much time we have, even if we live well. Even if we live one thousand years. I believe that in the eleventh month of the nine hundred and ninety-ninth year, we will say, "where did it go? I'm not ready yet." So, I respect time now. Not scarcity. There's plenty of time, but no time to waste.

Lesson #2: *Everyone is making it up as they go along.*

No one, and I mean no one, knows what they are doing and anyone who pretends to have it all figured out is young, delusional or lying. The way to prove this to yourself is to ask the person next to you right now, "Is there an area of your life where you are holding a question?" The people who feel like their career is dialed, often worry about a spouse that they haven't really connected to in a long time. The people who feel that the partner is good might instead be worried about the kids. The people whose kids are good wonder if they've missed doing something in their career. It goes on and on.

Holding a question, and death, are the great equalizers. Also, as you get older, more skilled and comfortable, you start to notice that the very best in any category are responding in real time from a place of curiosity and confidence in their ability to figure it out as it arises. Even when they use deep experience and precise expertise, they are making it up as they go along because any specific instance of life, problems, participants, have similarities but are still different.

So, if everyone is making it up as they go along, then if there's something you want to try or do, just do it.

Lesson #3: *The best way to learn is by doing.*

If you had met me in 2015, and you were an investor, I would have peppered you with questions on investing because I had a dream in my heart of using capital to spark the building of the type of tech that I believe in. I took a seminar on venture capital in 2016 that resulted in a big investor saying, "I'll put in $100,000." But I didn't start right then because I felt I wasn't ready. That I didn't know enough yet. So I took more seminars on investing, read more books and blogs on investing, and went to conferences on investing—without investing.

In 2021, I co-founded a venture fund and learned more in one year of actual investing than in 6 years of getting ready. That has taught me that whatever you want to learn, just do it. It's the best way to learn. And since everyone is making it up as they go along. And you have less time than you plan. And there's plenty of time, but no time to waste. Just do it. If you want to learn if you like something, just do the actual thing, and you'll find out fast.

But *how?* Out of all the things that can be done, how do you decide what to do?

Lesson #4: *It's not about the destination, it's really about the journey.*

Here's another lesson that takes age to grasp. For every goal you set, what do you think is on the other side of that goal? Another goal. And on and on and and on. It never ends. And then you start to notice that everyone who goes from goal to goal to goal is kind of miserable—often surrounded by failed marriages and relationships of all kinds. Also, as you realize this, you begin to question the point of the 'goal' as an end point. So what is the point?

Goals are important to know if you accomplished them and need to measure them so you know what you did and by how much. But, the goal itself is not the point. The point of a goal is how it transforms you. Did the goal require you to meet new people, do new things, or go to new places? Did you learn? Did you grow? The goal is just the lattice for the transformation.

I recently started following Dan Sullivan, the OG coach who

coined 10x as easier than 2x. Often people hear that and think it means work 10x harder. It does not. It's really about picking goals that require you to transform. If you pick a 2x goal that you can easily accomplish and you already know all the details, then it's not a goal that will change you in ways that allow you to experience more of your life.

When seen this way, you can move on from going from goal to goal like a little hamster, to a deep rich life where you move to experiencing transformation after transformation. Plus, you might as well pick the 10X goal anyway—it's far more interesting because you'll learn what you need to do by doing it. Remember, everyone is making it up as they go along anyway. And you have less time than you've planned for your precious life.

Lesson #5: *Since it's about the journey, how that journey feels is what matters most.*

How do you want it to feel? Do you feel alive? Connected? In integrity? Does it light you up? There's a difference between easy and easeful. Very "hard" things can be easy—working long hours by day and getting a PhD at night—when you feel alive and are being transformed by the goal. Very "easy" things can be torture when you are not aligned—listening to one more voicemail from a boss who you know lacks integrity. Learn to know what you're feeling, and if it doesn't feel right for you. For me, I want to feel authentic, connected, and alive.

Lesson #6: *You are a creator and have the power to change what's around you to feel the way you want.*

Anytime a situation, internal or external, doesn't feel the way I want it to feel, I believe I have the power to create new conditions. First I ask, what is unsaid, unowned, unasked, undone? Then if I get an answer, I say, own, ask or do the thing that came up. Afterwards I check, now, how do I feel? Or I see if there's a bridge I can lay down to greater connection to myself or others. Something else I've come to understand is that people are facing so much loneliness. If you offer a bridge they will pole vault across it. We're all longing for connection. My coach Joe Hudson says, "Connection, Connection, Connection." Meaning if you start and end with connection, and if you do the action be it business or love from connection, then the likelihood of things working out is high. Connection and the trust it creates makes everything easier.

Lesson #7: *If the way something feels won't shift, even if you do, then it's ok to leave.*

I no longer feel the need to finish books, stay to the end of a play, or answer a question just because I was asked. Whether it's a job, a relationship, or a friendship—if my taking responsibility for myself doesn't shift the way it feels to what I want to experience, then I own that it's ok for me to leave. Your life is precious. You have plenty of time, but no time to waste.

This is what I know to be true.

—

Nichol Bradford *is a pioneer, innovator, investor and thought leader at the intersection of technology and human transformation.*

Jacob Notlöv

There is no Other Way I Can Make Sense of it All

What can one know to be true? I was introduced to Immanuel Kant in high school and our teacher did a very good job at using Kant's teachings to create a full blown existential crisis for me. I found it interesting, baffling and very annoying to not be able to say anything for certain. It's ironic to remind myself of Kant, a quarter century later, through Chat-GPT, an AI tool prone to hallucinate in a way that sounds unequivocally true.

I guess that it's been my life process to mature into a person that accepts the loose constraints life has to offer. During—and for many years after—high school, religion and spirituality were clumped into a bucket of sloppy thinking and old people's desperate attempts at redemption. I saw practitioners of faith as the ultimate cop outs, not daring to stare into the darkness of existence, void of any comforting stories of paradise, oneness and forever more.

Can one exist in a purely atheist way? I was brought up with a caring and passionate mother who showed me a humanistic way of living and caring for others. While I thought I could use clinical deduction and a critical mind to navigate life, my norms from my upbringing clearly formed my underlying beliefs, dogmatic truths and ideology. Long after growing up I can see that much of my early dissonance came from holding two world views simultaneously: A nihilistic, performance optimising, cynical and hedonistic worldview on one hand and a humanistic, energetic, feeling and faith centered way of life on the other hand.

While contradictions are fascinating and a great starting point for self discovery, mine nearly consumed me multiple times during life. I've found it very frustrating to deal with the pursuit of what is true for me, while not feeling consistent with that which isn't clearly defined, explained or understood inside. There is something inside. Something that speaks faintly but ever more clearly when listened to.

You are mine, so very mine to listen to, my voice, my little whisper. A faint tremble, a wave delayed and an extra sway in the wind.

You are me, my voice of will, push and pull. That ideal, deep below reason and ideas. A strength from faith unaccounted for.

I am. So very much. Much more than I could ever think of.

I started writing poetry a few years ago. Mostly in Swedish and typically after some alcohol and an inspiring chain of events. There was something between reason and feeling. Letting go while still holding hands with that beautiful consciousness of mine, supporting a flow of words to come out in just the right order. I would write on little pieces of paper, throw them away and sometimes even let them burn. Not saving or sharing what I wrote, made it irrelevant if it was good or useful. Doing something for the experience of having done it felt sacred. Like a celebration of experience and existence.

Intuition and authentic feeling in contrast to thinking and understanding has been my path to know more things to be true. My typical process is to understand something through exposure, trial and error and conversation. If a dogma, ruleset, approach or idea stands the test of logical scrutiny I'm still hesitant to see it as mine. It can be useful and something to refer to as a thinking pattern but for something to be inherently true for me it needs to be felt through practice and intuitively resonate when used.

I guess the slow adoption of new dogma and thinking patterns is how we grow older and transition into something new. I feel new and different, especially when I visit places from when I was young. I remember my thinking patterns from before and how it felt to be that person. With a bundle of dogmas disguised as absolutely unequivocally righteous truths.

I like my mind more now. I like to disprove myself and to be surprised by my own sometimes magnificent ignorance. I guess slight illusions of omnipotence and a pinch of narcissism come with being a young human. Something needs to make us think we can change the world and do better. Just as acknowledging the loose constraints of life come with growing older.

If all dogmas and ideas can be challenged and falsified. If there is no heaven and forever more. If the use of reason is just my biological neural network ticking away in my head. *What remains? What is true?*

Can all the layers of the onion be peeled away with nothing of substance left behind..? Is this even the right question to handle for me as an entity? My mind with it's 'me, myself and I'... Referring to oneself from and with itself, thus acknowledging that there is a starting point, and going back to Kant—the real philosopher.

Theory and history aside. Aside from dogma, religious or otherwise, logic, from experience or deduction, there is something more that is true for me. It's the end result of 'I do this X activity because...' I want to maximize or optimize something. And that something at the very end of a long sequence is... *survival,* which includes procreation. And its language and expression is love.

Life itself must be understood through love and care. There is no other way I can make sense of it all. It's that one goal at the end of every sequence. And from that one starting point we can expand in all directions. I also think that something feels more true when the steps away from love are fewer. It doesn't need meddling, translation or description. Expressions of love are easily understood across culture, age, gender and language.

Love is something we all strive to give and receive, growing with each exchange. This is what I know is true and some of the twists and turns of how I got there.

—

Jacob Notlöv *is an Entrepreneur & CEO at No Paper Menu Ltd.*

Bob Chapman

My Journey from Management to Leadership

The story of my 50-plus-year career in business is a story of transformation. It has taken several decades to reach what I know to be true today: leaders with the courage to care truly make a difference at work and that everyone matters! From being a traditional business leader focused on achieving success—defined by money, power and position—to becoming a caring people-centric leader dedicated to stewarding the lives in my span of care.

This transformation, inspired by a series of 'revelations' that began in the late 1990s, changed my view from seeing the 13,000 people in our organization as 'functions for my success' to seeing each of them as someone's precious child. Simply stated, I went from focusing on 'me' to devoting my life to creating a world of 'we'. This transformation laid the foundation for my vision of a world where leaders embrace the profound responsibility of leadership. They then focus on creating environments where people feel valued and have their dignity affirmed through their work which they carry home and treat their family, friends and neighbors with that same sense of care. This is how we'll create a world where everybody matters!

Our leadership model—which we call Truly Human Leadership—has been validated by the exceptional growth in human and economic value in Barry-Wehmiller, as well as the growing global interest in our message. In 2015, we released our book, *Everybody Matters: The Extraordinary Power of Caring for Your People Like Family*, which details my transformation story. The book has sold over 110,000 copies in seven languages. Harvard Business School also wrote a case study about the Barry-Wehmiller culture, now taught in more than 70 universities.

Our transformation journey has helped us see that business could be the most powerful force for good in the world if we have leaders with the skills and courage to care for those they have the privilege to lead. By sharing my story, I hope to inspire others to embrace these principles.

I received a very traditional business education with a bachelor's degree in accounting and an MBA in business. After graduating, I spent two years as a CPA with Price Waterhouse before joining the family business, Barry-Wehmiller. From my education and early business experience, I came to view success in life as the accumulation of money, power and position. This view of success caused me to be very 'me' focused.

In 1969, I left PW and accepted my father's offer to join Barry-Wehmiller. At that time, BW had $18 million in revenue. The company had been around since 1885 when Mr. Barry and Mr. Wehmiller launched it to build equipment for the brewing industry. By the early 1950's the company struggled to compete in the global brewery market. At the time, my father, who worked for Arthur Andersen, became the auditor for Barry-Wehmiller and, during an audit, was offered the role as treasurer by Mr. Wehmiller. Shortly thereafter, the Wehmiller family wanted my father to find a new owner by working with an investment banker, but no one was interested in the struggling business. In the early 60's a lending organization agreed to lend Barry-Wehmiller the funds to buy out the Wehmiller family stock and my father became a 60% owner with the $30,000 investment he had made in the 50's. Thus, Barry-Wehmiller became a Chapman Family company and has remained so to this day.

My first six years with BW became a self-designed leadership development program that began with a role in the engineering department and eventually roles in customer service, manufacturing and international license agreement oversight. My first real leadership role came when my father suggested I take over a struggling small tool and die business that we owned which proved to be a great challenge and exceptional hands-on learning experience for me.

In 1975, six years after I joined Barry-Wehmiller, my father passed away suddenly at age 60 and, literally overnight, I found myself president of a struggling $18 million dollar company with fragile financial performance. The sudden loss of my father, combined with our banks wanting to pull our line of credit, resulted in a significant challenge for me at age 30. However, that challenge motivated me to improve the financial performance of the company and use the tools I learned from my education to cut costs and quickly improve earnings to pay down debt.

Next, I initiated dramatic strategic technologies in the exciting new fields of solar energy, electronic inspection and filling to complement our historic brewery equipment. Revenue from these new initiatives grew over four years to $72 million and it seemed like we had created an exciting new future for our company.

Unfortunately, those innovations failed and, when combined with a decline in our historic brewery market, created a major financial challenge in 1983 that resulted in our bankers pulling our line of credit. For nine long months, we operated with a daily focus on cash. We were within inches of bankruptcy. In hindsight, both the 1975 and 1983 financial challenges were exceptional learning opportunities that provided the foundation that shaped our future.

A pivotal year in our history was 1984 when I came to the realization that, although proud of our history, our past did not give our stakeholders a future. So, I set out to acquire other companies to get us into markets with a better future. We have now completed over 140 acquisitions (or, as I like to call them, 'adoptions') around the world. That path created a diversified $3.5 billion global organization that has experienced over a 10% compound growth in our share price with a future that will be shaped by additional acquisitions as well as healthy organic growth.

Up until around the year 2000, our financial success was driven by a robust business model shaped by traditional profit-creating leadership actions. But in 1997, I began to experience a series of 'revelations' that profoundly reshaped the way I looked at my role as a leader and became the principles of Truly Human Leadership.

The first revelation occurred in 1997 after we acquired a $55 million business. I was there the first day of our ownership and it happened to be during March Madness, the NCAA Division I men's basketball tournament. I was getting a cup of coffee in the break area before the day began and noticed the excitement and fun people were having, talking about the office pool and which teams would make it to the final four. In hindsight, what I witnessed was people having fun and then, when it came time for them to start working, you could just see the fun go out of their bodies! This became my first revelation: Why can't business be fun? Why do we call it work? I began to implement games that were aligned to value creation with an individual component and team component each week. Once we launched this unique weekly motivation program, we saw a 20% increase in revenue and a 1,000% increase in fun and joy among the team! And, we saw a dramatic improvement in customer service. As one team member said, "I always thought I was nice to the customer but now I am really nice because I want to win!"

The second revelation came at our church where the rector was an inspiration to our family. One day, after a great sermon and service, I looked at my wife Cynthia and said, "Ed [the rector] only has us for one hour a week but at Barry-Wehmiller we have people in our care for 40-plus hours a week!" As I walked out of church that day, I realized the powerful influence we have on the team members within our span of care.

The third and most significant revelation was at a wedding where I was experiencing the joy of the families of the bride and groom and the friends gathered. Everyone was focused on how precious this bride and groom were. Suddenly, the lens through which I saw the 13,000 people in our global organization was completely reversed. Rather than seeing them as 'functions for my success', I saw each of them as someone's precious child who was in my span of care for 40 hours a week. The way our organization treats our people has a significant impact on their health and how they treat their family and friends. The way we lead impacts not just the way they work but the way they live! I realized our true purpose is our *people*—not accountants, engineers, hourly workers, head count or labor!

These three revelations built on one another to shape my emerging sense of purpose as a leader. I believed that I had been blessed with a profound message that could heal the world and I didn't want it to die with me. We needed to create disciples who would embrace this vision of leadership and carry it beyond my time. We gathered a group of team members and developed our unique curriculum inside Barry-Wehmiller with the intent of creating leaders who had the skills and courage to care for those they had the privilege to lead.

The initial curriculum centered around three principles of leadership. The first was a class to teach the skills of Empathetic Listening to help people listen to understand and validate others, rather than listening to debate or judge. The second was to help our leaders focus on Recognition and Celebration, things Cynthia and I had studied in detail while raising our six children. We learned that you need to catch your children doing things right five times more than identifying things they did wrong. Adults are identical in needing feedback! And finally, we developed a class called 'Culture of Service', which focused on seizing every opportunity to serve others.

These classes were critical in moving Barry-Wehmiller from a me-centric organization to a we-centric organization. We provided them through our internal Barry-Wehmiller University to take our leaders on a transformational journey from management to leadership. At many of the graduations, I have been deeply touched when participants share what they learned and how these experiences impacted their lives. This question frequently brings tears to many of these adults as they realized those they had unintentionally hurt as a 'manager' at work and at home. No one likes to be managed!

When we began teaching these classes globally, we saw that the impact was universal. No matter where you are in this world, everyone wants the same thing: to know that who they are and what they do matters. Ninety-plus percent of the feedback was about the impact our classes had on their marriages, and relationships with their children and family. Up until that time it never occurred to me that the way I would lead Barry-Wehmiller would impact our team members' personal lives!

When learning about the transformation underway at Barry-Wehmiller, business leadership author and speaker Simon Sinek visited our facilities to meet our people and experience our culture firsthand. His reaction was this: "I am no longer a nutty idealist, for if it exists it must be possible!" Simon was so profoundly touched he wrote about BW in his next book, Leaders Eat Last, and continues to be one of our biggest advocates.

After similar reactions from visitors from Harvard, McKinsey, and other organizations, we were urged to share our message which we have done through Everybody Matters, the Harvard Case Study titled *Truly Human Leadership*, my TEDx talk and speaking engagements to audiences around the world.

Through our work to encourage other leaders and organizations to join us on this healing journey, we have come to this incremental realization: Why is there such a need to teach leaders how to care? We believe our educational curriculums provide students with the academic skills the market desires, but are not effectively teaching students how to be leaders as they progress from a technical role to a leadership role. Today, we have begun initiatives to transform educational curriculums to integrate human skills with academic skills to create tomorrow's leaders who have the skills and courage to care.

Our message of *Truly Human Leadership* is gaining significant interest. We are encouraged by the leaders who are stepping forward to begin to heal the poverty of dignity we are experiencing in every part of our society. We are guided and inspired by our vision to move from a me-centric to a we-centric world where everybody matters!

This is the world I imagine and will remain my focus until it is the norm!

—

Bob Chapman *is Chairman and CEO of Barry-Wehmiller*

Jason Lippert

The Power Of Caring For People in Business

At a listening session recently at my company, I was reminded how amazing business and people's results can be when everyone is promoting healthy culture, leadership and the pursuit of personal and professional goals. At Lippert, one of our company goals is simply to make sure every human being that works here has a personal and professional growth plan, that it's written down, and that they share it with someone! All the way to the front lines of our business. This is extremely rare to find out in companies these days, especially in manufacturing companies at the front lines of the business. That said, I feel that connecting people to purpose and personal and professional goals is part of the cure to healing the broken world we live in today.

We simply feel that working on your personal and professional life in an intentional way by setting goals in these areas gives people a deeper sense of purpose at work. Accomplishing these things through a personal and professional growth plan helps our team members grow, it impacts the growth of their team and business and, most importantly, we've watched it impact their families at home as they are growing by accomplishing these personal goals. So, for those reasons it's a huge focus because of the amazing impact and transformation it's having on people's lives. Impact that keeps people wanting to stay for the long term.

Since starting up several different businesses here, leading people through our transformation and having experience as CEO of a $5 billion public company, I've learned so many lessons and so much about people but there is one thing that I really want other business leaders to learn—it is that the power of caring for people in your business in a courageous and selfless way will produce more results for people and your business than anything else you could ever do.

The single most important metric in any business is likely turnover. Why? Because the quality of people and the frequency those people show up to work with over months and eventually even years, determines the good or bad outcomes of four key areas of the business: safety, innovation, quality and efficiency/productivity. A business cannot have high quality results in any of these four areas if the quality of caring for people is low and the frequency of turnover is high. Simply, the higher the quality of living your team has, the longer those passionate people stay—this outcome will ultimately determine safety, product or service quality, the likelihood of innovation and ultimately how effective the workforce is.

I learned this the hard way, by trial and error over the years. For the first part of my career, me and my team focused only on the outcome and how much we were winning. The more we won, the more successful we felt, the more we got rewarded by our board, investors and Wall Street in general. Until, one day, about

18 years into my career, I started feeling empty. While I felt the leadership team and decision makers were winning in business, we didn't feel like we were winning in LIFE. I started praying… and praying. Over the course of that year, there was a lot of prayer simply asking God what my purpose was (it couldn't possibly be growing a business and being successful in the eyes of business people). The answer came through a TED talk I heard called *Truly Human Leadership* by Bob Chapman—the story of how Bob woke up and realized that through the power of caring, we can not only achieve better business results, but we could impact people's lives and change the world. God spoke to me through that inspirational video that's now had millions upon millions of views. I ended up connecting with Bob through my good friend Justin Maust (a staunch healthy culture coach), and after spending a few hours being mentored by Bob, we launched into our own culture journey, which I believe is having a significant, positive world and human impact.

What I know to be true is that you simply can not impact or transform people nor the decision they make to stay or leave the organization without a powerful, consistent and effective culture. After 30 years in business, I'm convinced that this kind of culture is the only way that leadership can influence turnover in a meaningful way. People simply won't stick around if the company's values aren't visible consistently throughout the organization. And this, I can say with experience over the last 10 years, is very, very hard to do. Without great culture, it stands to reason that a business can not be great at safety, innovation, productivity, and quality can not exist in the best form. It's simply not possible.

The reason over 80% of businesses fail at executing great culture is because great culture never takes the front seat. Leaders of businesses consistently put profit first and sacrifice or ignore values altogether in an attempt for a bigger bottom line. After all, that's what we were taught in business school. Manage expenses and manage people. One problem though, I don't know a single person that likes to be managed, supervised or bossed (I learned that from Bob Chapman). Organizations are missing a few key things. First and foremost, they need a culture department. I don't know why companies expect to have a great culture when they make it 'everyone's responsibility' or HR's responsibility. Organizations don't give the sales function to everyone, or the HR function to everyone or IT to everyone for that matter. No, they give it to champions or leaders in these fields that can organize and execute key priorities in these areas and who drive regular action and solutions to problems. Most companies give culture to HR and that's almost laughable. HR was a very overloaded function 20 years ago and today with DEI and all the social issues and opportunities and demands on that function, they couldn't possibly take on culture, which most business leaders refer to as the 'most important thing in my company.' Protecting the values of the company needs to be someone's job and the CEO or top leader simply can't go out there and make it happen in every square inch of the business on a consistent basis.

I would encourage any business with approximately fifty team members or more to think about having someone lead culture and values for the business. The fact that any business would show an interest in having a director or VP of culture or any type of culture leader speaks volumes about how the company thinks about and values culture.

At every interview, I ask the potential candidate we are interviewing, "did any of your last companies you worked for have a Culture chief or someone over top of the culture dept?" The answer almost every time is "no" (and usually accompanied by a snicker). When I tell them we have a whole department around culture to help our company organize and coach our people around what it means to live out values AT WORK and how we hold people accountable to those values, corporate philanthropy and community service, chaplaincy, leadership training all the way to the front lines of our manufacturing business, dream achiever programs and life planning, and so much more, their usual response is complete disbelief and that it sounds simply too good to be true.

So this is the opportunity for you and your company. People don't expect their company to pour into them in a meaningful way and I ask the simple question: "which team member/employee (I dislike that word but am using it for a broader audience) would you rather have. The one that is getting poured into by a culture team through the filter of great values, one that we are engaging in setting goals for their personal and professional life and teaching them how to lead themselves and/or their team better, or the one that just signs up for a pay check and to do the job—a team member that ultimately will come to the job, not get poured into and likely just look out for him or herself because they certainly don't expect the company to do that. I know which one I'd take.

Up to this point, all the benefits seem to be for the company, but this is where this concept of 'Conscious Capitalism' or 'Business being a Force for Good' as my good friend Bob Chapman and I call it, comes into play. Ready for it?

The real benefit of truly living out a genuine culture founded on good values that are followed and upheld consistently is that your people will be happier, healthier, more trusting of leadership, leading themselves better and leading others better—all which creates a world more like the one that God planned for us in the first place.

Team members that trust the company and its leaders will bring more passion and energy to work than companies who put values on the wall and rarely follow them. Good culture is the only way to have truly engaged team members and having truly engaged team members will always be a competitive advantage over competitors or peers that don't have engaged team members. You can't have poor culture and good engagement. The two simply can never go together. It's an impossibility.

When we teach and live values at work and help team members in the business develop personal and professional goals, and walk with them through that never ending journey, the end result is that these men and women start leading themselves better and most importantly, go home and lead their families better. This is the holy grail of great culture. Families are better equipped, they have a better chance of success. This is the ultimate result waiting for businesses and business leaders everywhere—the power to create better family units in our communities. It stands to reason that if for 40 hours a week (or more), a team member is around solid, consistent values and leadership, the more of that they will take home if taught. If they are taught to lead people or themselves better at work, they will lead themselves and their family better. No one can argue with that. When kids and families start growing up in these healthier, leadership and values rich environments, the world starts to look just a little bit better. But we can't change it until more businesses truly put values first. Bob showed us, we have shown others and those others will show yet others. The revolution has started and companies cannot turn their backs on this because if they do they will eventually not have any team members coming to work.

You have to trust me that team members who feel valued, trusted and that can count on a consistent culture built on solid values, will ALWAYS do more and bring more passion, energy, innovation, quality and safety to the workplace than someone that doesn't feel like there is a good culture or trusting leadership. That isn't such a large assumption now is it? So I will ask again. Which team member would you prefer? Of course the one that is bringing passion and energy to the job, but you can't have that until you have the cultural foundation set first.

Ultimately what I have learned over the years to be true is that we are simply talking about loving your people and when we do that, you will have a business that is truly acting as a light and a force for good in this world.

—

Jason Lippert *is President and CEO of LCI Industries (LCII), a global manufacturer of components and engineered solutions for recreational vehicles, marine and transportation industries.*

Eda Çarmıklı

Paying it Forward

I believe we are navigating through both intense and fascinating times—a unique blend of profound light and deep darkness, marked by individual awakenings and global conflicts. While we increasingly acknowledge our interconnectedness as one human family on Earth, we still struggle with dilemmas, prejudices, and injustices. This, I've come to understand, is the dance of the *Law of Polarity*, a fundamental principle of creation.

I once envisioned a world beyond this duality, where each individual is awakened and actively contributing to a better world—a vision our collective hearts know is possible. Yet, as I journeyed through life, I recognized that this perfect awakening might be more an ideal than a reality. After all, our very existence is birthed from duality and hence, everything in the universe exhibits duality. Light and darkness, often perceived as opposites, are essentially identical in nature but vary in degree. Consider water: whether as vapor or ice, its essence remains unchanged. This principle applies equally to all those that are seemingly opposite; they share the same essence but manifest differently. It's our perception, our illusion—*maya*—that labels them and defines them as good or bad.

However, I did not give up on my innate belief for Utopia and seek refuge in the *Law of Vibration*. The creation operates on mathematical principles, and everything, including our thoughts and emotions, vibrates at a frequency. For the last 8 years, I have first handedly experienced that we can raise our personal frequency by choosing our circles—our *we*—deliberately, aligning with the energies we wish to embody. Cultivating an ecosystem of higher consciousness, I discovered that it's possible to resonate at higher frequencies, such as courage, acceptance, reason, love, joy, and peace. This is how we can rise above the confines of polarity and embrace a more expansive existence.

Living in a world governed by polarity, it's the conscious awareness of the *Law of Vibration* that empowers us to shape our own realities. This insight has been a guiding light for me, illuminating the challenges as valuable lessons in life. Despite the complexities and contradictions of humanity, by mindfully choosing my immediate tribe, I often experience—and even physically feel—glimpses of Utopia in my everyday life.

As I witness the collapse of old systems, I find myself uncovering new layers within and challenging established norms. My dedication to my personal growth and actively contributing to global awakening serve as my guiding compass. Perhaps it's inherent in my nature, I can't be sure. But, I've never been one to dwell on complaints and gossip. Instead, my focus has always been on areas where I can truly make a difference, where my voice and actions can effectively influence outcomes. My intention has always been to be an active participant in life, seizing opportunities to realize my potential and initiate meaningful change that transcends the mundane and satisfies deeper aspirations beyond the mere gratification of the ego.

My Journey of Self-Discovery and Transformation

I was born in 1974 in Türkiye, at a time when the country was still grappling with modernization in the wake of Mustafa Kemal Atatürk's founding vision. My grandparents had witnessed firsthand the significant transformations he ushered in—from the separation of religious institutions from the government, the adoption of the Latin alphabet, to the rise of women's freedoms...

My father's side of the family is from Arhavi, a Black Sea village near the Georgian border. After losing their father at a young age, my uncle—the eldest of five siblings—shouldered the burden of familial responsibility. In 1966, he founded Nurol Holding, which is still the cornerstone of our family business. After my father finished his studies in civil engineering and married my mother—an architecture student at the time—he became a shareholder in the company's expanding ventures.

We spent my first years in the southern city of Iskenderun, where Nurol really began to carve out its niche in infrastructure and construction. Soon life blessed me with a sister, Ceyda—born just a year after me, who has remained a pillar of companionship and support throughout my life. In 1985, our family expanded further with the arrival of my brother, Ozi. Together, as a tightly knit family and extended group of ten cousins, we have been navigating the complexities and opportunities tied to our family's legacy amidst the ever changing tides of Türkiye's unfolding history.

The later years of my youth were spent in Ankara—the country's capital and bureaucratic hear—which significantly shaped my character. During my primary school years, a sense of loneliness often enveloped me, as I struggled with the social dynamics around me. This urged me to become an observer, always trying to understand the intricate social constructs around me from a certain distance.

After years of introspection and seeking to understand my true essence and purpose, I now see why I was the way I was. I always felt a bit like an outsider, identifying myself as somewhat of a gypsy, slightly hippie, or, in today's terms, maybe even a little 'witchy'. My quest has always been to uncover life's deeper meanings, to understand societal norms, the concept of value, and the intricate dynamics of human relationships.

After finishing my degree in Business Administration, I moved to Los Angeles in 1996—accompanied by my sister—to pursue my further studies. This period was a time of self-exploration, detached from my usual routines, where we embarked on a journey to understand our true selves, our personal limitations, and the direction of our life paths. Upon our return to Turkey in 1999, although I sought to apply my abilities to work with creative minds, out of a desire to please my family company's legacy I gave in and entered the corporate finance world for six years.

Even in the thick of that process, I could not resist the pull of my spiritual journey that had started to take firm root in Los Angeles with yoga, breath exercises, meditation, and silent retreats. These powerful experiences led me to become one of the founders of *The Art of Living Foundation* in my country, marking the beginning of a lifelong commitment to my personal growth and outward service.

For quite some time, like many others, I struggled for balance between these two worlds, and ended up following the predetermined path of societal norms, getting married and welcoming my daughter, Maya, into the world. Yet, I was clearly able to see how the competitive and respect-driven corporate way of life was in direct conflict with my personal values and beliefs. Since I had always dreamt of being a mother, I decided to seize the opportunity to leave my career for some time to be present during my daughter's formative years and savor the joy of watching her grow.

After much soulful debate, when I finally decided to return to the real world I chose another path. I joined a boutique real estate development consultancy company, Servotel, with the intention of making a positive impact on sustainable architecture and improving quality of life through thoughtfully designed shared physical spaces. This experience served as an enlightening introduction to decentralized systems, compassionate leadership, and the empowering nature of collaborative work. However, the harsh reality of investor-driven decisions and the prioritization of profit maximization over vision often made me question the true impact of our efforts.

During these years, at the age of 39, I started experiencing panic attacks that shook my reality. Despite meeting all expectations of life, I found myself on unstable ground, feeling profoundly lost. The familiar airplane safety phrase: "Secure your mask first before assisting others" started to resonate deeply with me, both literally and metaphorically. The phrase actually became a turning point, leading me to prioritize myself and reconsider my path even more deeply. I found solace in words. Writing my *Believer In Life* blog provided a space for my self-expression and reflection. At the same time, I embarked on a 200-hour yoga teacher training, with Chris Chavez, to reserve some intentional time to listen more attentively to my inner voice and explore the depths of my being. These steps were not only about finding stability; but, also about redefining my relationship with myself and the world around me. The most transformative moment of my life occurred in 2016, with a diagnosis of papillary cancer. This experience brought a stark realization that life is too short and none of us will leave this world alive. This was reflected to me in a profound saying by Mahatria: "This is the only chance you get to be you, please do not miss yourself". It was a call for me to embrace this singular life, this unique existence I have in this body, born into this particular story.

This realization gave me the courage to leave my job, redefine my marriage as a lifelong companionship, and pursue a life of authentic purpose and alignment. It was during this difficult time that I found the bravery to speak my truth, which transformed my relationships and eventually ignited the entrepreneur within me. It was as if the wizard inside had been brought to life. Instead of seeing my illness from a state of victimhood and self-pity, I viewed it as a chance for profound introspection and re-birth. It was a calling to finally express what had been simmering inside me for a long time. My sickness was a blessing in disguise.

The moment you accept what troubles you've been given,
the door will open—Rumi

During that unprecedented period, it was through a 'Pay it Forward' initiative on Facebook that Markus Lehto, my partner, entered my life. His curiosity, joy, multi talentedness and wisdom were not just companions, but beacons that guided me. His unwavering belief in me and my words inspired me to confidently take center stage of my life, both figuratively and literally. Together, we founded Joint Idea, Love Mafia, and Life Works Labs, embracing our heart's desires and rewriting our narratives. Our path over the years has led us to extraordinary collaborators —dreamers who act, seekers yearning for a better world. Today, we are proud to be part of many inspiring communities like the Corporate Unplugged Forum, celebrating the power of collective action and shared vision.

As fate would have it, my relationship with the family business, which I once kept at a distance, has also started to flourish again after my journey of self-discovery. Today, I find myself actively engaging with it, not out of obligation, but with joy and a desire to make meaningful contributions. I am currently involved in the creation of our Family Constitution and in fostering alignment within the Family Council. My entrepreneurial initiative, Life Works Labs, allows me to merge my worlds beautifully. I have the unique opportunity to touch and inspire employees of our family company. Moreover, it is a great honor to be working alongside my sister in shaping the Sustainability Department within the Holding company. This role gives us a unique opportunity to positively influence our corporate culture.

Your task is not to seek for love, but merely to seek and find all the barriers within yourself that you have built against it—Rumi

Through the highs and lows, and the confrontations with life, I've come to understand that life is inherently rhythmic. Everything rises and falls, following its own cycle. Life, in its essence, is a school where we journey through phases of experimentation and error. These cycles often persist until we transform them with comprehension, leading to transcendence. It's through this process that we break free from repetitive patterns, evolving with each lesson learned. Every experience, every cycle, is a step closer to understanding and expressing our true selves. They are opportunities for healing, for inspiration, and for growth.

When You Have More Than You Need, Build A Longer Table Not A Higher Fence

Throughout my life, the philosophy of Paying it Forward has been my guiding principle. This ethos became particularly clear during a period of silence at the Bangalore Art of Living Ashram in 2001. I always wondered about the disparities in life—why some are born into wealth and others into hardship—a teacher's words in the ashram struck a chord in me: "If you are born into this life with wealth and love, where life's challenges are met with compassion, then you are here to pay it forward." This insight was a profound revelation for me.

At our core, we are all fundamentally alike, each of us equipped with one body, two hands, two feet, and the same 24 hours each day at our disposal. There is a limit to the material possessions we genuinely need or can use. These profound words have become my life motto. When our cup overflows – whether it be materially, emotionally, or spiritually—it is our duty to channel our abundance into serving the whole. This realization reshaped my understanding of life's inherent system and about my direction in life. It's not just about what we accumulate, but how we use our fortunate life story to make positive contributions to the world.

Paying it Forward is much more than a simple act; it embodies the universal law of cause and effect. Our each decision and thought acts as a catalyst, setting in motion a wheel of consequences. In today's world, where scientific exploration delves deep into the quantum realm, we understand that our choices – whether to react or respond—initiate a chain of multiple realities.

In life, I have witnessed that choosing kindness, empathy, and support not only heals the other but also increases our own wellbeing. After all, we vibrate what we authentically are. When we embrace this approach towards life, we not only initiate acts of goodness but also set off a chain reaction of positive outcomes. Love Mafia, the main force behind my unwavering belief, is the result of these intentionally and compassionately woven connections.

Every decision (action) we make triggers a corresponding outcome (reaction) in our lives and the lives of others. Rumi's words, "Yesterday I was clever, so I wanted to change the world. Today I am wise, so I am changing myself" stand as a very true reminder that the true change (reaction) begins with a change within ourselves (action).

As I reflect on my own journey, I recognize that each belief and thought (cause) has shaped my path (effect). Now I see that embracing my vulnerabilities and courageously expressing my truth was not just about my personal growth but about setting a chain of positive outcomes in motion in my life. Like a Phoenix rising from the ashes, I emerged more insightful and hopefully wiser, influencing my surroundings with my words and actions.

The Way Forward with Universal Laws

I believe that understanding and respecting these universal laws is crucial for us to evolve in life. We should never forget that the nature of our causes will always determine the nature of our effects. With our response we can create a ripple effect of positive change, starting from the inner self to the outer world, embodying the principle of Paying it Forward in every aspect of our lives.

Beyond right and wrong, there is a field. I'll meet you there—Rumi

This profound quote by Rumi is the focal point of my approach to life, that supports the Pay it Forward perception. It underscores the importance of transcending beyond the need to always be right. Acknowledging the validity of others' perspectives, accepting that each one of us is right in our own view allows us to move beyond the ego-centric *I* and enter a space where we can collectively contemplate a future that prioritizes the *we* over the *me*. I believe that, in this shared space, free from polarity, we can foster a more inclusive and compassionate world.

It's not just about being responsible or ethical; But, understanding the profound impact our thoughts, decisions, and actions have on ourselves and the world. As we journey forward, I hope that we can do so with the awareness that each step we take is a cause setting a chain of effects in motion. In the cosmic dance of life, leading with awareness, insight, compassion, and wisdom can pay it forward for generations to come.

—

Eda Çarmıklı *is the co-founder of the global collaborative platform, Joint Idea; Life Works Labs; and Love Mafia community. She is also a second-generation shareholder in Nurol Holding, an industrial conglomerate in Turkey operating in construction, infrastructure, machinery, energy, investment, banking and tourism.*

Rebecca Henderson

Learning to Teach in New Ways

The Climate Crisis in my Classroom

I have recently come to understand that I do not know how to 'solve' the climate crisis.

I have ideas, of course. But the more work I do in this space—the more time I spend supporting students and practitioners in thinking about these issues—the more I realize quite how ignorant I am—and quite how poorly prepared those of us who work in higher education are to deal with it.

We could double down on the stock in trade of much modern climate education: technology and policy. This seems both important and insufficient. Should we not also be teaching something about where the social movements come from that drive policy? Something about implementation? How do we teach something so embedded, so qualitative, so human? Can we teach students to see the whole, when our training and our thinking is so fragmented, so often focused on a small piece of all that is happening?

How can we help people learn to hold their despair, their rage, their feelings of impotence? To learn to tolerate their emotions with tenderness and patience? Can we teach hope? Is hope what we need, or do we instead need to teach the power of doing what must be done because it must be done?

Can we help our fellow humans discover that there are fates worse than death and goals much more worth striving for than wealth and power? That the climate crisis could be a door to a much juster, much more alive, much more connected world? How do we give substance to the idea that we are not only competitive, selfish beings, but also connected, cooperative, loving—and dare I say transcendent—beings? How do we make such views feel anything more than naive, wishful, *dangerous*?

Through philosophy? Moral education? Living examples? Can we compete with a culture that is all encompassing, all appropriating, infinitely fluid and deeply cynical? Is compete the right word? *Do we need an entirely different way in?* What do we know about finding allies and companions, building community? About finding joy, when it will never be 'all right' and there will be so much suffering? *What would teaching look like if these were our goals?*

I do not know the answer to these questions. So I find myself, week after week, in a small basement classroom with 24 students, teaching—and listening and singing, laughing and wondering. We eat barely warm vegetarian pizza in the breaks. And we are trying—with love and gentleness, and with fear and despair, too—to learn together. I have never done better work, and I have never felt more uncomfortable and unsure. It is a great gift.

Over and over, I ask myself: "What would you do if you were not afraid?" And then—then I try to do it.

—

Rebecca Henderson. *Author, John and Natty McArthur University Professor at Harvard University.*

Charles O'Malley

Unlearning as a Path to Truth

I recently saw a question posted on Facebook: "What is the driving force in your life?" Some had said: compassion, love, joy, hope, kindness… It took me only a moment to know my answer: *truth*.

I have a paradoxical relationship with truth. It's easy to equate truth with knowing, or the knowledge of something. Increasingly, though, I have come to understand that truth is much more closely related to not knowing—and so I find that searching for truth is more to do with *un*learning than learning.

In my teens I remember asking myself the question: "How do I know what is true?" I came into the world as a light-skinned male towards the tail end of the 1960s, born into a middle class, British, Catholic, conservative family living in a wealthy suburb of south west London. In my teenage years, I attended a private, Catholic boarding school and Thatcher and Reagan were setting the dominant tone of the political context in the social circles I belonged to. So, as we all do, I grew into a particular set of values and a set of social, political and economic perspectives. I absorbed a certain view on truth: the way things are and the way things should be.

As I followed my search for truth, at some point in my teens, I came to see that if I'd been born into other circumstances, my worldview and my most firmly held beliefs and truths would have been completely different. How then could I have confidence in my own truth as opposed to anyone else's? What is truth in this context? How could I ever know what is true? Does it even make sense to speak of truth?

Much of our political, social and economic discourse takes place in the form of a competition between truths. My truth is better than yours. If we pause for a moment, it doesn't take long to appreciate the socially constructed nature of much of what we take to be sacrosanct. If you'd been born to a different family, in a different place in the world, in a different culture, or at another time in history, you would hold radically different positions to the ones you currently hold. When we are able to see and understand this, we can relax our attachment to our truth and our own reality and become curious about how others see and experience the world.

Aldous Huxley's book The Perennial Philosophy, which I read in my 20s, explored the writings of all the major religious traditions and showed that beneath the surface-level, doctrinal differences, each of the major religions was pointing to a deeper-level, universal truth. Many paths, but one mountain. We can apply this approach to other areas of life, whether that be debates on economic and political systems or on the hot topics of the day: climate, immigration, inequality, and so on. On the surface there is much that divides us on these issues, but when we go further on the path, we begin to touch on common hopes, common desires and common values.

Occasionally I organise 'Connected Conversations' dinners at which each diner receives a conversation menu, as well as a food menu. The conversation topics are questions for discussion that are designed to foster deeper connection between two conversation partners. One of my favourite questions for these conversation menus is: "What is a core belief you hold that may not be true?" I realise that in effect I have been asking myself this question for much of my life and, as a result, many of my core beliefs have fallen away over time. There are the more obvious things, like belief in specific religious doctrines or particular political points of view. Then there are the much more subtle things that we typically don't see and are completely unconscious of, because they make up the water we swim in: the dominant worldviews, narratives and ways of seeing in our culture. As Alan Watts said: "We seldom realize that our most private thoughts and emotions are not actually our own. For we think in terms of languages and images which we did not invent, but which were given to us by our society."

In my experience, a person's strength of conviction often seems to be negatively correlated with their connection to truth. When a person is overly attached to their own ideas, it becomes impossible for them to see or hear anything else. Journeying towards truth is about giving up what we think we know and becoming open to not knowing. A process of unlearning, rather than learning. This is likely to expose us to waves of discomfort, uncertainty and fear: it can feel a lot safer to be certain and to take a stand in a particular tribe. But, there is a deeper wisdom and greater possibility that can be found in not knowing.

In the food and agriculture team at the United Nations Development Programme (UNDP), where I work, a current conversation is whether we should take a stronger position advocating for agroecological approaches to agriculture, or whether we should be more neutral, helping to bridge between different perspectives and positions. I appreciate the value of standing for something, of taking a point of view, of holding a position. I support campaigning and advocacy organisations who explicitly make this their mission. Evolution progresses through the dance and interplay of polarities and there is an aspect of evolution that is about struggle and competition. In that context, taking sides is important.

However, I also think that there is a crucial role for those who seek to connect across divides, who help us to see and understand different perspectives and what connects us, beyond what divides. To me this is central to the ideal of the United Nations and why I believe our role is to connect people across our differences and to hold our own positions lightly and with humility. Ultimately there is wisdom to be found within all perspectives. The insistence that we all agree on a dominant narrative can marginalise those with other points of view. If people feel unheard for too long, and if they feel that their perspective is ignored or disrespected, then over time they will become increasingly radicalised. In 'Deep Democracy' facilitation practice, it is precisely the fringe and marginalized voices that we listen out for, because often it is there that we will find the greatest insights about what really needs to be attended to: what others are seeing that mainstream opinion may be blind or deaf to.

Rumi said: "Out beyond ideas of wrongdoing and rightdoing, there is a field. I will meet you there." For many of us, this is a heretical place to go. We are all for taking a position in order to identify our place of belonging and which tribe we are loyal to: which football team, political party, or which side of any polarising political debate. Politicians, political opinion and political correctness would all have us insist on moral absolutes and accuse those who refuse to do this as being the enemy, by default. However, when we become less dogmatic, when we let go of separating people between the good and the bad, allies and enemies, we discover not moral relativism, but rather greater openness and compassion. Our perspective broadens and so does the space of what is possible. In this place, the possibility of getting unstuck increases and the possibility of healing and reconciliation improves. Conversely, sticking to our truths and insisting on our rightness can often just lead to never ending cycles of conflict.

When we get to the further reaches of not knowing, we enter territory in which it becomes hard to express the form of knowing that paradoxically resides there. As it says in the *Tao Te Ching*: "Those who know do not speak. Those who speak do not know." Connection to truth becomes more experiential than cognitive; more mystical than rational. To communicate these ideas, I find that I turn to poetry rather than prose. In my poem below, I describe it as *A Strange Kind of Death*, because it involves a fundamental letting go of who you think you are, and the ideas and truths that you hold on to for security and belonging.

There's a strange kind of death,
which beckons you like a lover,
seducing you
towards exotic palaces
you don't know how to find.

Your mind tries to remind you
of other apparently safer paths.
But a thirst for something other
than what you know
pulls like an irresistible force
of remembering; indistinct
memories of a time
before you took up residence

in your parents' house, when
your womb was darkness
and you didn't know why
or what it was to form
defences.

Your heart is obedient
to a deeper longing
that draws you home, while
everything you thought precious
is retreating from you.

Even as a distant whisper
reminds you to reach out
for all the ideas you were given
to build your life upon,
in the overpowering silence
your arms have become dumb
and forgotten movement.

So, instead,
the dream of knowing fades
and a space beyond you
quietly watches
as everything drifts away,
and you, sweetly weeping,
melt into an embrace
that cannot be spoken
or explained.

The poem speaks to a radical spiritual surrender into not
knowing. A place beyond all stories. This is where I have arrived
at in my life and I hope it's a place which will help me to be more
effective in my work of bridging and facilitating across divides.
A key part of this bridging work is to help others relax a little

their attachment to the stories they hold. We are in a time when our attachment to 'all the ideas you were given to build your life upon' is becoming highly problematic. Our attachment to certain ideas of how the economy must work—as a perpetual growth machine—is eating up ecosystems, destroying species, and tipping the biosphere dangerously out of balance. We take as non-negotiable certain ideas of money and the financial and economic system, when in fact these are largely socially constructed fictions. We sacrifice at their feet the much less negotiable biophysical reality of how life operates on this pale blue dot of a planet.

To survive and thrive through the rest of this century and beyond, we will need to come up with radically different ways of organising ourselves as a species within the broader web of life. The first step towards this is to see that many of our fundamental beliefs are fictions, once convenient for organising society, but now increasingly misaligned with the maintenance of a favourable environment for many species now alive on this planet, our own species included. When we relax our certainties and step into not knowing, then a far greater space of possibility and creativity opens up. We get beyond out-dated and unhelpful, polarising debates. We can begin to listen to each other more genuinely, to meet each other more fully, and to discover wisdom in the most unexpected places. The truth about the universe is that everything belongs here, everyone has a place here and, if we can get beneath the surface appearance, we see that every perspective carries some form of universal intelligence.

—

Charles O'Malley *is a Senior Systems Change Advisor, United Nations Development Programme UNDP. His work focuses on strengthening collaboration to address complex global challenges.*

Neha Sangwan

Life **Lessons of the Heart**

Every interaction, experience and relationship offers important lessons for us to grow, heal and connect more deeply—to ourselves and each other. Ultimately, discovering our own Life School path requires us to learn how to turn up the sound of our heart—slightly louder than we can hear the voices of others.

—

When I was born a mere 18 months after my older sister, Ritu, my Indian immigrant parents both needed to work full-time just to make ends meet. In our culture, extended family raising children is commonplace, so my grandmother (affectionately called Nani) came to live with us. Then came the plot twist: The United Nations offered an assignment to my grandfather (Nana), and he requested that Nani join him. So Nani scooped me up and, together, we headed to Kenya to support Nana's new adventure.

Two years later, my mom and my sister Ritu arrived in Africa to bring me home. At such a young age, I didn't know how to cope with my sorrow and pain. I cried in protest for nearly a month. No matter what my parents said or did, they couldn't soothe me. I figured I must have done something wrong to be taken from my Nani and Nana. I wasn't the only one exasperated. Ritu wasn't happy either. At the ripe age of three-and-a-half, she was being forced to share the parental love she had been enjoying all to herself. That's when the bullying began.

Even though I didn't realize it, I was willing to do whatever it took to please those around me, so that I wouldn't be sent away again. I subconsciously enrolled in my first life school course: People-Pleasing 101. I began focusing exclusively on my external environment, becoming hypervigilant about what others expected from me—and then, giving it to them. Doing whatever my sister commanded? On it. Academics? All A's. Athletics? Top singles player on the tennis team.

When I was seven years old, I overheard my dad on the phone with one of his friends saying, "Yeah, just my luck, the second one was a girl too. I was hoping for a son to follow in my footsteps and become an engineer." My knee-jerk reaction was "Oh no! Dad wanted a boy? At least I'm good at math and science, so maybe I can become an engineer."

In parallel, my mother mentioned how she missed her calling to become a surgeon. She would say, "Neha, if you go to medical school, I'll join you!"

I became the queen of overriding my own heart, making it my mission to fill the unfulfilled dreams of my parents and grandparents. The day I figured out that engineering and medicine weren't mutually exclusive, I knew what had to be done. Yes, it's true. I'm a mechanical engineer and an internal medicine physician. (Don't be too impressed, that just means I'm a really good Indian child). In an attempt to belong, I never considered what my own heart was saying. I had disconnected from my body and ignored the desires of my soul from a very early age.

What about you? Were there people in your life that you desperately wanted to please? Have you made education, career or relationship choices based on your desire to fulfill someone else's dreams or expectations? If so, don't beat yourself up. This lesson often occurs when you encounter a different course in Life School—Belonging 101.

For each human being, belonging is a primal need—as important as food, air and water. That's why sometimes we get confused about what really matters—to us. And rather than following the signals from within us, we make choices to find that sense of acceptance through achievements such as:

Money —the numbers in our bank account
Fame —the stats of engagement on our social media posts
Power —where we are located on the organizational chart
Accomplishment—degrees, medals and awards

Achieving what we think will please others often results in a short-lived satisfaction—followed by unexpected feelings of emptiness and disappointment. We may find ourselves stuck in a pattern of dissatisfaction, anxiety or depression. Sometimes, this discomfort and pain can seem like the end of the world; it's not. Instead, it's actually an important wake-up call, a detour of sorts—redirecting us to the real lessons we are meant to learn—the ones that bring us back to listening to our own heart.

—

If you're curious about the difference between whether you're on your own path or following someone else's, ask yourself a few questions:

1. What's an important goal you hope to achieve?
2. If you were to achieve that goal, what would it give you?
a. Does achieving this goal bring you joy?
b. Or is it more about what will bring someone else joy? If it's someone else's joy, what would satisfying them give you?
3. When you achieve your goal, pay attention to how long your satisfaction lasts?

—

Over the next thirty years, mastering the art of people-pleasing with my sister, parents and grandparents served me in my work life as well—as I met all my hospital efficiency metrics, received exceptional patient satisfaction scores and had the relief of not being named in a lawsuit.

Boy, did that lesson from childhood serve me…until it didn't— because our childhood strategies aren't meant to last a lifetime. Pain surfaces when we outgrow them. And the good news is—we can graduate! At some point in adulthood, we face a conflict, a crisis, or a major stressor that is like an entrance exam to the graduate studies of life. And we either fail and keep facing it again and again or we pass and actually start to grow and expand (mentally, emotionally, relationally).

Three years into my tenure as a busy hospital physician—fueled by sugar, caffeine and a fear of failure—I burned out. On medical stress leave, my only goal was to get well enough to return to work again. I wanted this crisis and my "perceived failure" to be over. I didn't think there was any other choice.

I began my burnout recovery by doing whatever it took to save myself from falling off the cliff and losing or leaving my job. In the weekly sessions with my psychiatrist, Roger, he explained the key role that stress played in burnout. To my surprise, I also learned that the research shows that stress causes or exacerbates more than 80 percent of all illnesses.

Physically, I had been experiencing severe throat constriction and insomnia. But rather than partnering with my body, I pushed through it. After listening to my story, Roger made the connection that my throat constriction was one way my body communicated that I was holding back and wasn't speaking my truth. All it took was me paying attention. I had never connected my physical body's signals with my fear of failure and my desire to belong. The next time throat constriction occurred, I recognized the pattern. Almost reflexively, I found myself reaching for a Mountain Dew, because the carbonation soothed my throat and the sugar was so comforting. This is when I became aware of how I had been overriding my throat—such an important physical clue.

Burnout Life Lesson #1: *Decipher your body's physical clues and pay attention to what they're saying.*

Your body is talking. The question is are you listening? If you find yourself feeling depleted and sensing it's time to make a change, two practical steps will provide awareness about what your body is telling you.

Step 1. Tune in and decipher your own physical intelligence. Expand your awareness from the external world to also include sensing your internal world, the physical signals coming from inside you. When you get out of your comfort zone—do you notice your heart racing? Stomach turning? Shallow or deep breathing? Is your jaw tight? Your muscles tense or relaxed? When you treat the physical signals and messages coming from your

own body as important data, you become aware of what you
need.

Step 2. Identify your coping strategies. These are creative ways you
have adapted over time to cope with stress, deal with challenging
emotions or avoid conflict.

There are so many creative ways that humans use to push
through the physical signals of their bodies—whether it's fatigue,
pain or even throat constriction. Some other common coping
mechanisms include:

Sugar-Caffeine Buzz Strategy
Chocolate-Makes-Everything-Better Strategy
Glass of Wine (or three) After Work Strategy
Retail Therapy Strategy
Sleep-It-Off Strategy
Doom-Scrolling Social Media Avoidance Strategy
Exercise-It-Off Strategy
Work-Even-Harder Strategy

The problem with coping strategies is that they're only a
temporary solution that doesn't solve the underlying problem or
address what your heart is trying to tell you.

This brings us to an important point. There are multiple ways to
solve a problem, so it's important to know on which level you're
ready to embark:

Option 1—Averting a Crisis
Option 2—Staying Afloat
Option 3 —Healing the Root Cause

Here's what each of them entail:

Are you interested in a quick-fix to save yourself from an

emergency? If so, Option 1—Averting a Crisis is your best bet.

Would you like coping mechanisms that allow you to remain in the same situation? If so, Option 2—Staying Afloat seems like a good fit to buy you some time.

If you're ready to address the root cause of the issue, that would be Option 3—Healing the Root Cause and learning the lesson that life is offering you. The good news is if you choose this one, you will learn important lessons that serve you better than your old strategies.

Upon reflection, I can now see that while on medical leave, I was mostly interested in Option 1 (Avert a Crisis)—physically recovering from the acute crisis so I could get back to work. Roger pointed out that the goal of my time off wasn't to return to work as quickly as possible. In fact, it was meant for me to slow down and reflect upon the ways I'd been functioning that were no longer serving me. This was paid time off to discover new ways of relating to myself and my work. Somehow his 'permission' helped me relax. If I was going to return to the hospital and didn't want to feel so depleted again, I needed to develop some new coping mechanisms that would replace my sugar-caffeine buzz strategy. So I advanced to Option 2 (Staying Afloat). I reduced my working hours to 80 percent to reduce stress and still remain financially stable.

As I began journaling, I realized that when the hospital leadership deliberately chose not to create a staffing back-up schedule for sick calls as a way to save money, my strong sense of duty to my patients motivated me to volunteer for all open shifts to ensure there was adequate coverage. During one of our sessions, Roger discovered that a significant portion of my stress came from me single-handedly trying to fill in for the chronic staffing shortage. This was another wake-up call. I began to reflect on whether my mind-set was helping me or hurting me. Was this just how I was wired? Maybe that's why I went into medicine; it's primary focus is on taking care of others. As time progressed, I got curious about myself and my motivations, and sensed that change may be on the horizon.

I remember the day I was called to the emergency room to re-admit a patient for yet another heart attack. It was then that I realized I was not solving my patient's issues, I was band-aiding them from one crisis to the next. I didn't want to do that anymore. I wanted to leave my role as a hospital physician, become an entrepreneur and heal the root causes of illness (which I now knew were largely due to stress) decades before someone ended up in the emergency room. That truth terrified me. If I left practicing in the traditional medical system: *Would I be abandoning my patients? Would my decision cause conflict? How could I give up a lifetime of job security? Could I actually pave a new path in medicine? Were there others who would join me? What if I had to face failure again? And most importantly, what would my parents, my grandparents, my colleagues and my boss say?*

I found myself at a fork in the road. Once again, I could feel myself sliding toward the slippery slope of burnout. My energy was low and my heart heavy. This time, I recognized my physical signals and their related emotions.

It was time to listen to my own heart, trust myself and surrender to the unknown—Option 3 (Healing the Root Cause). This is where real growth occurred because I had to trust myself enough to take a risk and move beyond awareness to action. I learned how to draw boundaries and value my own self-care so that my body got good sleep, felt nourished and most importantly—heal the underlying trauma that led to my people-pleasing. My fear of doing something wrong, not belonging and getting sent away again had driven my actions for long enough.

Rather than fearing separation and avoiding my emotions, I

began to view every interaction, experience and conflict as an opportunity to grow and heal. This time I was the one leaving—taking the leap and letting go of what no longer served me and making this decision, aligned from the inside out. One of the most unusual things happened. A sense of clarity emerged. Even the muscles of my throat relaxed.

Armed with a sense of personal power, I found the courage to leave the hospital and became a speaker, author and entrepreneur—transforming stressful cultures into healing organizations. I wanted to help people identify and address the root cause of their stress long before they ended up in the emergency room. In fact, rather than hurting my work relationships, the very hospital system I left hired me back as a consultant to coach their physician and nurse teams on stress management and communication.

Burnout Life Lesson #2: *For any important decision, make sure to turn up the sound of your own heart louder than the voices of others.*

This shift in me also fueled growth and healing in my relationships. I asked my parents about the years I lived with my grandparents and the statements I'd heard them make when I was young. Those conversations opened my heart to what was happening in their lives at that time. I gained an understanding of how they made their decisions and discovered that they had no idea about the painful impact it had on me. They also had never intended to pressure me to go into engineering or medicine; they weren't trying to make me do something that I didn't want to do. They were just voicing their own missed opportunities, regrets and pain.

By being brave enough to have these discussions, I actually felt closer to them and it expanded how I viewed the path and meaning of my life. I began to see an alchemy at the intersection of people's desires and dreams—like my parents' and mine—and discovered how these moments shape the course of our lives and the choices we make. I did have choices along the way. I longed to feel valued, loved and appreciated by my family and my community. I finally owned that I made those choices in an attempt to belong.

After burning out, I dedicated myself to figuring out what I wanted and especially what my body and heart were trying to communicate with me. Every choice I had made led me to who I am today: An engineer who valued root-cause problem-solving; a medical physician who understood there was more to physical health than just numbing physical symptoms; and an executive coach who addresses health across physical, mental, emotional, social and spiritual levels.

Burnout Life Lesson #3: *Own your choices and get curious about the people and experiences that influenced you.*

Be kind to yourself as you evolve. These lessons can take months or years to integrate consistently in your life. Awareness is the first step to expanding your perspective. Growth and healing come with repeated application of what you've learned. These days, my throat serves as a reliable companion to signal when I'm not speaking my truth and warns me not to slip back into the pattern of giving up my own needs to please others. I know I've graduated from this life lesson, because as soon as I acknowledge my body's signal and shift course, it gently subsides.

I assure you that, if you pay close attention and study the lessons that present themselves over and over, you'll heal your past and be able to connect deeper with those who have influenced you the most.

What I know for sure is that each time we choose not to learn a lesson, to perhaps avoid it, ignore it, or eat, drink or numb our way through the discomfort, the lesson only returns—bigger, louder and more intense than before. When we just want a conflict, dilemma or challenging situation to be over, we miss the opportunity to learn our lesson and get stuck in using strategies that perhaps our younger self relied on. If so, we'll likely be repeating that class in Life School again. And since we'll be learning until we die, rather than repeating the same lessons over and over, wouldn't you rather fill your life with the adventure of growth, healing and more meaningful connections?

—

Neha Sangwan *MD, Executive Coach, Wellbeing and Communication Expert, Author, Speaker, CEO and Founder of Intuitive Intelligence Inc. consulting firm transforming stressful cultures into healing organizations*

Karin Volo

The Joy of Receiving in Life

One of the many things that I know to be true from my own life experiences is that we need each other. We need people who love and care for us that we also love and care for as well. We need to be able to give AND receive. Many people are givers—it's easy for them to share their time, energy, support, love, and give to others. It can also be very difficult for these people to receive. I know because I was one of them!

Notice the past tense. Yes, I had a big lesson in learning to receive. At the beginning of 2023, I was quite ill and didn't really understand why or what was happening to me. I'd never been sick in my life and kept thinking to myself this will pass, I'll get better soon. How often do we ignore something only to have it get worse? It got to the point where I ended up in the emergency room because I could barely breathe and walk. Literally! My lungs were filled with over five liters of fluid! After a couple of weeks with a battery of tests showing my chest filled with rapidly growing tumors, the doctors finally diagnosed that I had a malignant stage four non-Hodgkin's lymphoma cancer. I quickly realized I couldn't do this alone!

The shock and then the rapid pace of treatment information was hardly digestible, and the daunting task of having to figure out how to tell everyone in my world was overwhelming. Honestly, I didn't really give myself time to be scared but rather went into project management mode. I frantically started writing lists.

They say you find out who your friends are in a crisis and I was incredibly touched by how many people wanted to help. In the beginning of this journey, I needed to figure out how on earth I was going to organize all the people who wanted to help me? Then I imagined circles like a pebble dropped into water. The most inner circle was my family. My daughters and I cried together and I needed to reassure them that I would make it through this. Then I had three close friends who were able to support me from a more spiritual perspective. Next, I had a Power of Eight group (I can highly recommend Lynn McTaggert's books and research on this concept!). I would work with this group on specific intentions, requests, and healing. Then I had a few different gratitude groups and communities that were keeping me in their prayers and positive thoughts. I would regularly post updates and make specific requests for prayers and healing in these 'hubs' that were then shared out like ripples to the groups as needed.

The hardest person to tell, however, was my 85 year old frail mother. She had already lost her husband and two children (to cancer and suicide), now her last living child was facing this! I was so afraid she wouldn't be able to handle it. My mother has always been strong during a crisis, she has been my rock many times when I needed it. And it was only after the life storms passed by that she would break down herself. Yet she'd been through so much and life had taken its toll on her over the years. Would she have the strength to make it through this? The women in my family tend to be strong, courageous, and resilient. I was relieved to see that she had accepted the situation and would find strength, even though we both knew we were scared.

So many wonderful people stepped up to the plate to give support in whatever ways they could. Having been on the other side of watching a loved one battling cancer with both my father and sister who both eventually passed, I knew it was easy to feel helpless, not knowing how best to help someone in need. You want to do something but there really is not much that you can do. But in addition to my loving family, many of my dear friends helped me in very practical ways to get through a very difficult period in my life.

From the Corporate Unplugged community, I had lovely practical support specifically from some dear friends… Vesna was by my side with so much love and support, often sending small gifts and pictures or videos from her travels in Italy that brightened my days and inspired me to keep going. Geetali brought me warm home-cooked healthy meals regularly and took care of my little dog, Sasha, when I needed the extra help. Lesley helped me organize my winter/summer clothes and coordinated many friends to help fix my balcony with beautiful flowers to enjoy during the spring and summer. Ma went on a wild hike to find me fresh spring water and sent recordings of beautiful mediations she made just for me.

In addition, there were several other close friends who were instrumental in supporting my journey. Cindy organized a fund-raising page (because I lost a year's worth of income and my insurance didn't cover all my living expenses) where over 80 people (including some from Corporate Unplugged as well) generously contributed to helping relieve the financial stress

I would have otherwise had to endure on top of the cancer. Carina visited me regularly and guided me through the ins and outs of chemo and cancer since she had just recovered herself a year earlier, not to mention giving me the best goat cheese I'd ever tasted. Liliana was so active with her healing and spiritual insights, holding my hand virtually the whole way through and often giving suggestions on various foods I might need. Katarina was one of my biggest cheerleaders and always taking action to make things happen, like bringing me my healthy green juice to the hospital when I needed it. Hanna was so sweet to find the home-made corn tortillas that I was craving for comfort food and keeping me supplied during her loving visits.

Many other friends and colleagues simply kept me in their prayers and well wishes. An energy of shared love, values, and caring made such a difference. Learning to receive with grace from so many people in my various communities was a big lesson for me! I felt a web of love, and I felt cared for when I needed it most. And for that, I will be forever grateful!

Unfortunately, many people suffer in silence because either they don't want to ask for help or simply aren't even aware of how many people care for them. Why is this? This is something we need to seriously evaluate in our lives.

There needs to be a balance between giving and receiving and it's so important to learn to receive if you haven't. I REALLY had to work with this because I was so used to doing things on my own. During deep healing meditations, the common themes that came up throughout my life were the beliefs that 'I had to do it on my own' and 'I didn't feel safe'. I discovered that it was related to my father passing from cancer when I was ten and having to be so responsible at a very young age.

Despite these insights, it was still hard to be vulnerable, but it always touched my heart deeply to see how generously my dear friends and loved ones WANTED to help. I realized that if I did not learn to receive, I was denying them the ability to give back to me! There is a gift in both giving and receiving for each act of kindness. Like two sides of a coin, it's important to have a balance.

How did I find the strength to navigate and overcome cancer? One of the biggest tools that was so helpful that I deliberately worked with (and continue to this day) is gratitude. Almost every day, I wrote down a list of things I was grateful for and then I would share it with my gratitude groups. I wrote my gratitude list on the notes in my phone, then simply copied and pasted it to five or six groups in WhatsApp. I was already in several of these gratitude groups because it's a process I had been practicing for a couple of years, thanks to my dear friend Marc who got me started.

Gratitude became a lifeline. There were the 'tough days' where I really struggled, I didn't feel well, nor did I have the energy for anything much less to write anything about gratitude. Going through chemotherapy took a huge toll on my body. There were so many side effects that I could not even begin to imagine. The utter exhaustion where I could barely get off the sofa, various reactions to different drugs, the numbness in my hands and feet (neuropathy) which made it difficult to balance and to even walk, dozens of blood transfusions were all very challenging. I even broke my arm in the middle of the treatments when I slipped on ice on a walk with my dog! And then there were the sudden life threatening infections because the immune system was so suppressed due to the treatments. Reading other people's gratitude lists honestly helped sustain me through so much!

What I've learned is that there are four levels to gratitude, each of which requires a deeper experience when working with it deliberately.

Thinking about gratitude activates oxytocin in your body which helps you to stay positive and feel loved. It also helps to create neural pathways that make it easier for you to see good things in life.

Writing down gratitude moves gratitude from a thought and feeling to activating the more logical parts of your brain. This helps to process emotions and make things more concrete.

Sharing my gratitude list with others meant being vulnerable which was challenging in the beginning because people would read such personal things about my life. But I quickly got used to this one as I observed how it quickly led to deeper connections and a sense of love, friendship, and support. My gratitude groups vary from 2 to up to 10 people participating.

Reading others' gratitude lists is where magic really happens for me because I got to see other's lives through the 'Lens of Gratitude'. It has lifted me up on a dark day and created deep connections.

Once I got used to sharing gratitude, it became addictive—in a good way! It was FUN to do this process and it became one of the most important 'tools' that I embraced during my cancer journey, specifically because I could read people's lists and also focus myself on things I could appreciate each day. Seeing lives through the Lens of Gratitude reminds me that we are all humans having challenging life experiences but that we can always find things to be grateful for regardless of the circumstances.

Gratitude is a magical emotion that can lift us from despair to joy in an instant. Using gratitude as a tool is a way of giving back to yourself and training your mind to see the beauty in life. It is also a gift you give to others. Many friends regularly comment on how inspired they have been after reading my gratitude lists. Seeing a difficult cancer journey through the lens of gratitude has helped others realize they can get through their own challenges as well.

On a sunny summer day, I had the final meeting with my doctor to go over the last extensive x-ray. The doctor was so happy to share that I was officially cancer free! A wave of relief, tears of joy, and immense gratitude washed over me even though this was the outcome I had been expecting all along. To have it confirmed by the doctor and x-ray dissipated those small nagging doubts that played with my mind. I had gone through six tough months of intense chemotherapy, plus several other strategies working with integrated health (I won't get into that here, but I share in my Living Your BEST LIFE program if you are curious). Having so many people sending healing and prayers, and working with daily gratitude, my tumors disappeared and I was given the gift of continuing my precious life and bigger purpose of bringing joy! My perspective changed to truly see that my life was filled with miracles. We only have to see them.

There were many lessons for me during this cancer journey: the ability and joy of receiving, the importance of having a strong community, understanding our deep connection, and the essence of loving each other. And most of all, I learned to love myself unconditionally, which is still an ongoing endeavor.

Being willing to receive unconditional love from others—and from myself—is truly the joy of receiving in life!

—

Karin Volo *is the CEO of Evoloshen, Trusted Cultural Advisor & Strategic Partner to CEOs & CHROs on Culture & Creating High Trust Teams, Chief Joy Bringer, Inspirational Speaker.*

Vesna Lucca

You **Are the One I Have Been Waiting For**

We all carry feelings around that influence how we react, how we look upon life and how we make decisions. If we become aware of them, they will instead become signals that guide the direction of our path.

I share with you my journey of profound loneliness and divine togetherness and how—by dancing with both—I understood what I needed to heal. This is a story about how the intrinsic power of loneliness became a dynamic force in my life that pushed me to learn, and to actively seek out my context and my peers, and find new paths towards my purpose.

—

I always had a deep sense of loneliness. Since as far back in time as I can remember. Running through the woods with my friends, I would suddenly get pulled into a bubble where time had stopped. Petrified, I held on to my breath until the freezing wind of loneliness passed. There are no apparent reasons for it, but it's always been there. Sometimes very visible, at times hidden away. Since it did not create any major life issues, I learned how to live with it by avoiding connecting with it deeply. I was great at being busy.

My twenty plus years of career life was filled with achievements, exciting opportunities, discoveries, as well as learnings—often sourced from a line of challenges and disappointments. Like getting a huge responsibility at a very early stage of my career, but with lack of guidance and clarity from the boss. Later on, the challenges were more about the lack of integrity and backbone in leaders. But at the same time I was immensely grateful for my life, travelling to South and Central America, South East Asia, and Southern Europe from my base in the US. Everywhere, from Jakarta to Bogotá, I was welcomed into my colleagues' families who made me feel at home. Wonderful people who opened me up to new perspectives and at the same time so much felt like the family vibe of my home country. I was in a good place in life. The new environments were challenging, but nourished my senses. Every now and then though, deep pain of loneliness paid unexpected visits.

I remember one Sunday evening, about an hour outside of Jakarta. I was in the backseat of the car, heading home. Suddenly, my driver slammed on the brakes to steer away from two young boys who appeared out of nowhere. We quickly jumped out of the car to check if they were okay, only to realize that this was a setup to get hold of a bag or money. They got away with some of it and, as an extra spice, left us with a flat tire. The driver left me in the locked car for a short while to get some help. Despite what had just happened I felt calm, present in a moment of unexpected total silence. I lowered the window of the car to get

air, peering into the pitch-black darkness outside. I closed my eyes
and took a deep breath. And there it was. This deep-rooted sense
of loneliness and abandonment. The pain in my heart was so alive
that I could hardly breathe. Tears kept running down my face. I
gripped the doorknob so hard my fingernails were white. What
was wrong with me?

These painful feelings kept coming and going when I least
expected them. Even my parents could not explain this in
any way. Could it be triggered by the fact that we had left the
comfortable life of my childhood Yugoslavia to start anew in the
far north, in Sweden, to gain the full freedom that my country
lacked at the time? Years passed by and the feelings of loneliness
never seemed to leave me, but I got really good at burying this
emotion.

I collaborated with wonderful people who shared the same
purpose at work. We were in flow and celebrated our victories
in creating good change. I was grateful, but also started seeing
a pattern in the contexts that would trigger the inner pain. Like
when power games and manipulation played out and innocent
people got hurt. This happened more frequently as I now worked
in the top layers of the corporate business world.

I recall a co-creation of a powerful company vision, only to see
it neglected as soon as a challenge arose. Even if I knew that
manipulation is fear based, it was disturbing to see lies, avoiding
taking responsibility and the crafting of words to get career
advantages. This led me to a new set of questions, like "why are
we morally obligated to do remarkable things?" My preliminary
answer was "because life is so difficult and challenging so that
unless you don't give it everything you have, the chances are very
high that it will make you bitter and then you cannot be a force
for good. Since you are all in, anyway, you might as well take
the risks that are adventurous. And there isn't anything more
adventurous than the truth." Eventually, I decided to follow my

gut feeling, to just say what I believe to be true and let go of the consequences.

Instinct guided me to allies and to leaders who welcomed me, leading from their heart, providing the oxygen to relentlessly continue my lifework journey. Again, I felt at home and embraced by this source of meaning. But over and over, like an unlikely storm, the force of change hit. Often linked to a new major owner of the company or a merger of companies or deep market shifts. Regardless of the reason, the powerful groundwork we had created and worked for, was abruptly washed away and the void was swiftly injected with power games and lofty visions. In several companies, I saw this cycle of build, destroy, and rebuild again repeat itself. So much value evaporated and so many people got hurt for no good reason. Did it have to be this way? The cycle of change.

A late afternoon, seven years ago, I was wandering through the royal gardens of Stockholm pondering my next steps. I stopped by my favourite old oak tree and leaned towards it to find myself hugging it. Like a dear friend I had not seen for a while. I was filled with a sense of calm, clarity, and insight as I stood there.

I took a leap of faith. I left the corporate world. I instinctively knew that now I could serve it better from the outside. I envisioned myself becoming an advisor to leaders who have the courage to care, who are committed to create a company that people love and respect. I felt at home. In addition, it would give me more time in Italy with my family and friends. Gratitude filled my heart. I was in the clouds, until my mind abruptly hijacked my joyful sensations with questions like: "How will you find these leaders? What if this is a lonely journey?" I shivered. My mind was probably right—there will be challenges. But, I still needed to do this. I owed it to myself, to life, to my inner voice that kept getting louder.

I mustered up the courage and exited the corporate highway. But it took a while to find my path. I found myself out in the woods where the colours were bright and the air clear. For a while, I kept looking from a distance at the highway where everyone else was racing and asked myself "what if my mind was right, this might be a lonely and confusing place to be with no immediate rewards to keep me on track?" I lit a candle to calm my mind and found myself transfixed, gazing into its dancing flame. A sensation of relief and freedom. I kept breathing deeply and let my thoughts wander like small fluffy clouds in the sky. Out of nowhere, my heart started beating faster, as an intense feeling of loneliness hit me. I don't know how many minutes had passed when I got out of this sensation and I found myself all wet with tears. What happened? Why? What is it that I don't get? I went to bed drained and confused.

The morning after, I gathered strength and decided to use my newfound sense of freedom to explore my natural interests that I had long yearned to pursue but never had the opportunity to deeply engage with.

I was immersed in the world of narratives, personal growth, leadership, the fabric of trust, the essence of heroism, the definition of success, while asking myself questions like "what does the world really need the most right now?" and "what could the future look like?" I wanted to create a method, using all the experience I had gained in the corporate world, to contribute to reinventing organisations through new ideas that were emerging. I started researching and found I was not alone on my quest.

I was completely absorbed by the insights found in books, articles, films, and documentaries that I kept attracting. They all held truths that I could recognize. My notebook kept swelling with reflections and truths that I savour. I knew I was on to something important, for me and for the people I was meant to collaborate with. I had so many existential questions in my heart that I wanted to explore with like minded and like spirited people. At the time, I did not know so many of them, but some. One of them is my wise brother who keeps reminding me, till this day, what a gift it is that I now can use my rich experience and fully explore conscious leadership—what it means to be fully aware of your role from a bigger perspective and to understand how all is interconnected—as a way to evolve companies into instruments for good change.

With time, I also dared to look into the intricate landscape of loneliness, exploring its deep-seated roots.

Perhaps loneliness is not merely a personal affliction but a symptom of larger societal maladies. Our modern era has generated a sense of disconnection and alienation. The prevailing narrative, with an emphasis on competition and the relentless pursuit of personal success, contributes to a profound sense of separation.

What if we come from abundance, and work together in community, instead of this idea that we are all separate? Most of us sometimes act from a place of 'there is not enough for all of us to go around'—not enough resources, power, control—instead of realizing that when we connect and work together from a feeling of abundance, there is plenty for all of us. There was a shift in me as I realized we can challenge the narrative and envision a society that embraces interconnectedness through compassion and cooperation.

While designing the soulprint method for companies, I kept reaching out to intriguing people around the world to compare notes with. As they one by one accepted my invitation to connect and talk and we realized how in sync we were, the subconscious shift from loneliness to togetherness started inside of me.

I kept attracting exactly the right people. Our dialogues and the

ideas of these brilliant people gave me so much hope and energy
that I wanted to share it with others, and shaped the podcast
Corporate Unplugged. Corporate because it was the instrument I
knew so well and wanted to evolve and Unplugged in order to put
the spotlight on the power of authenticity.

We all have potential within us to grow and move beyond what
is here and now—to be 'dreamers who do'. When we together
express a desired future and follow the backward engineering
steps—going from doing it as individuals to doing it as a whole
company team—we scale transformation, and it becomes a true
and lasting one. For this reason, I designed the Soulprint method.
A method that keeps evolving as I learn with others.

Gradually, through recommendation, leaders who were ready to
amplify their influence reached out. Together, we dove into the
deep sea, playing with their wildest dreams, rediscovering the
true purpose of the company, understanding their longing but
also the source of their challenges. Out we came with inspiring
opportunities, new ways to reach goals and a soulprint for the
company—a compass guiding people to take the right actions
and stay the course, in any weather.

It takes a lot of energy and deep conviction to go through
such profound journeys with these leaders. Where did it come
from? To see the glow in their eyes was enough for me to know
that we were doing the right thing. I have walked away from
collaborations with leaders who were not yet ready to fully
commit and stay the course long-term. It was hard, but the last
thing I wanted was to waste energy and time for any of us. Time
and time again—I learned to always come back and listen to my
heart and trust myself.

—

One beautiful autumn day, a new project brought me to Capri.

To the terrace of Villa San Michele, where the ancient Sphinx rests in its magnificent gardens. Perhaps it was the Sphinx who inspired my magical idea, to tap into the human algorithm and connect the extraordinary people I carried in my heart? I knew that if I brought them together, we would move mountains. A year later we gathered in that very garden in Capri. This became our Forum and extended family. The connection and trust were instant.

Through my experience over the past three years with my beloved Forum, and the trusted web of people around me, I understand now that I found myself in a haven that mirrored back to me what I needed to explore and understand about loneliness. I felt my power return, that I was carried back to my core to fully bloom and express who I am. To listen to the starry sky singing for me, showing me step by step the road I have chosen. I feel the presence of my ancestors before me, my dreams calling me, I sense friends and family around me. I see myself gracefully entering the world carried by all of them. I see how we are all expressions of the same energy and I say to myself:

I trust in the energy that you are.
I trust in the energy that I am.
We are flowing through each other.

Today, I know the source behind my loneliness and I'm learning how to embrace this wound and eventually heal it by realising I have all the safety, security and guidance within me. Once I have truly, and fully, embraced that, I am turning into a beautiful current of energy that shines throughout and around me.

It took to be in that forum group setting for me to see that I have all that I need in me. When I am ready to fully receive it, I can step into it and become a flower, spreading the seeds of intention.

The seed starts from a place of safety and security. The place we all know as home.

I was the one I was waiting for.

—

Vesna Lucca *is a Conscious Business Strategist. Advisor & Strategic Partner to CEOs. Founder of Corporate Unplugged Forum.*

Mia Bengtsson

Lion **Rabbit**

I am a lion-rabbit. Immensely brave on one hand, throwing myself into new situations and learning new skills, and scared to death on the other hand. When life becomes too much for me, I protect myself from the pain in the best way I know how: I move on.

This story shares an important revelation of mine, one that I believe may be familiar to many of you. That to develop the muscles of my heart, I need to stay and face situations where it is hard to love myself, where my ability to be patient and brave is challenged. That is how I grow. Allowing all the stories of my life—both good and bad—to play themselves out

I've always been restless. I need to see new places, meet new people, and learn new things, bearing my scattered resume as a badge of honor and bragging about having lived in five different countries. But it is only lately that I've come to realize that my high-achieving-never-sitting-still-always-ready-for-a-new-adventure lifestyle is holding something else. Something I've unconsciously tried hard not to resolve.

Growing up I often heard that I was too sensitive. I remember laughing and giggling a lot, but I also recall the tears. Lots of tears. Hurtful comments, to me or to others, upset me the most as well as any situation where children were suffering. I had a natural passion for people and a desire to understand them deeply. Despite being the smallest one in every group, I was a brave child, sticking up for myself and others.

I loved new adventures and fresh starts. I could daydream for hours about moving to a new country or meeting new friends. In every situation, the lion accompanied me, brave and strong, thriving in new situations. But always hand in hand with the rabbit, feeling scared and insecure. As a teenager, I was often the voice standing up for the less fortunate. At school the teachers would on purpose ask me to represent the weaker, less represented ones.

Most of my time I had my nose in books. Preferably Kafka and Dostoevsky. I wrote poetry and music. I gladly embraced the misunderstood writer or musician wearing the same color as I drank my coffee back then. Black. While I was a singer in a rock band and played the violin in another rock band, I was pondering whether to become a psychologist or attorney working for human rights.

Most of us have pivotal moments in our lives—when the world stops for just a second and there is this moment of enlightenment. As a teenager, I had one of those moments. I haven't always thought of it as a pivotal moment, rather a sad and difficult loss. But I've come to realize that the mechanisms I created in the aftermath of the loss became my safe haven that I am still to this day holding on to.

I recall sitting in my bed in my teenage room, doing some schoolwork for the next day. The phone rang. I didn't pick it up and instead slowly made it to my parents' bedroom. My brother came right behind me, and I could see in his face that he too had an uneasy feeling. My dad was on the phone, and I could tell from his tone of voice that he was talking to our relatives in the south of Sweden. I silently said a quick prayer for my uncle because all I could think of was that he must have had a heart attack. He had turned 50 the day before and to me anyone over 40 was considered old. My dad hung up the phone and after a long moment of silence, he told us that my 21 year old cousin had been shot to death. This was the first time I saw my dad cry.

In the aftermath of my cousin's death, I was dwelling even more on my misery and pain until one day I simply couldn't take it anymore. I decided to stop analyzing and live a lighter life. I started dressing in lighter colors, listening to different music, reading lighter literature, and having milk in my coffee. I even made new friends. I avoided difficult subjects and stopped taking a stand. For a very long time I felt good. I had stopped dwelling. I was always a high achiever, so I studied hard and worked hard. I created a life full of friends, travels, and meaningful connections but without a deeper purpose. Little did I know then that I kept avoiding my purpose, in fear of going to that dark place where I found myself after my cousin's death.

As a highly sensitive person, I certainly feel overwhelmed at times. But over the years, I have learned to use my sensitivity for something good; I can enter a meeting and read the vibes of the people in a heartbeat, I can trust my gut instinct and I know how to get along with most people. This sensitivity has also gifted me with emotional intelligence. Over the years I discovered my ability to feel deeply, which seems to bond me to people on another level. I often find myself in situations where friends and acquaintances come to me and ask for advice on difficult subjects. Having people around me who trust sharing their dreams, fears and troubles has made my life so much richer. This ability to bond and connect with people is a part of me that I've learned to cherish more and more.

Five years ago, I started my dream job. I became the CEO of a Family Office. Most importantly I found that their core intention—supporting entrepreneurs to make this world a better place by acting as long-term, responsible investors, treating people well—aligned with mine. My work gives me the freedom and the opportunity to have the most valuable and exciting talks in business. At times it also requires me to change direction in a heartbeat, which keeps me on my toes. My job has taught me the importance of longevity, in relations as well as in investments. For the past years my desire to make a difference and to stand up for people has begun to awaken and I am longing to find my true purpose. I can feel that something is holding me back and I keep coming back to the pivotal moment in my youth when I protected myself from getting hurt.

I've spent a lot of time pondering this 'purpose itch' and it raised many questions. I realized that, apart from my craving for meaning, I want an adventure in life that is so compelling that makes the possible misery of life not just justifiable but worthwhile. I want to be able to say to myself 'that was really difficult, but you know what, it was worth it'. So, the question is: where do I find the adventure of my life? How about in truth? Because I don't know what is going to happen if I tell the truth. It's a mystery. It means I have to let go of knowing what's going to happen. And at the same time, I realize that living out my own purpose and my truth is 100% me, and that is who I want to be. Why else am I here in this life? Whatever happens when I tell my truth is my adventure, my life. So my question to myself is: how willing am I to sacrifice something, and be willing to carry all the potential 'challenges' of my life? It would mean I have to let my narrow ego go enough so that I can voluntarily pick up all the challenges. And in doing so, it transforms me.

What is my truth? Do I have something to say that I'm not saying? If I do, then it is my fault and my problem. Well, I might be too afraid to talk. Fair enough, but how afraid am I not to talk? Why would I allow other people to control my tongue? If I try not to say what I have to say, I will be ok in the moment, but my life is so much more than moments. What am I ready to give up? Can I actively engage with the 'dragon' that burned me and practice this voluntary confrontation? Perhaps that stance then moves me forward into the world. Yes, that might work. My ponderings went on and on.

I keep returning to a wise story I heard some time ago about why we people are obsessed in the search for fundamental meaning:

Imagine two people laying bricks. They are building a gigantic wall, and the one person thinks: 'Oh my God, this is going to take 100,000 bricks, I'm laying one at a time and I'm wasting my life away trivially adding brick by brick to this gigantic brick wall, what am I doing? This is absolutely miserable'. Meanwhile, the other person thinks: 'In 300 years this is going to be a cathedral'. The person in the second state is doing the same thing, laying bricks. But, each brick is related to a very high goal and that means the reward is proportional to the goal of the entire behavioral process.

I want to be free to do what I want, but in a way that contains meaning. Once I define my true purpose, I'll need to make a change and unlearn my coping mechanism of moving on when the going gets tough. I realize more and more that to develop the muscles of the heart I need to stay and face situations where it is hard to love myself, and where my ability to be patient and brave is challenged. And that is how I grow my soul. Allowing all the stories of my life—good and bad—to play out. I'll also need to trust that I won't drown in my own feelings, which is a major challenge for me: To dare to let go and see what happens.

Finding my true purpose is a journey filled with questions and self-doubt, but also with curiosity and love. I trust that, very soon, I will be able to make the necessary changes to express it and embrace it.

After all, I am a brave lion, holding the hand of my life companion, the rabbit.

—

Mia Bengtsson *is CEO of Alsteron*

Liubov Shlapai

From **Chaos to Coherence**

February 23, 2022, is a date that I will never forget. More than two years have passed since I found myself on a desolate highway at the Ukrainian-Romanian border, cradling my one-year-old daughter and holding the hand of my other, just six at the time. The day before, just when the shelling started, I had sent my daughter to school, and we were the only family around us who dared to share the news about what was happening with our child. I had no idea things would be so bad so soon. What a difference a day made.

Beside me was Grandma, who was confused and going on about leaving behind her goat, cow, and blossoming flowers, but also anticipating a reunion with her son and grandkids in Canada within a few days. It was all beyond confusing. Just a few hours before that, a law was passed preventing men, including my dad, from leaving the country. We had no idea what was happening or what was going to happen. Our hopes, our dreams, our togetherness, and our whole lives changed in a flash.

We spent that day in a tearful crowd of displaced women and children, doing what we could to enter safe territory. Apart from holding on to my kids and our passports for dear life, all I could do was make dark jokes about how I missed the simplicity of Covid. At the time, it just seemed like God had a wicked sense of humor giving us a war as a reward for surviving the pandemic. It was, and still is, so surreal. I can't believe that we are still warring in the 21st century, especially with the country that called itself our big brother. How could this happen between people who were our friends, teachers, and schoolmates? Everything has turned upside down and inside out. Fear, stress, worry, and anger still mix uncomfortably with hope, responsibility, dignity, and love.

But, at least I am here to tell the story. At least I have a chance to create an alternative future for myself and my family.

We were amongst the lucky ones who could leave, but I have been burdened ever since by the guilt and shame of doing so. We girls were greeted anxiously by some Romanian friends at the border with the barely comforting words "we are here for you because we know we are next," as they put our small collection of luggage and worldly belongings into their car and drove us off to our unknown future.

Since that moment, every day has felt like a full week. While we ultimately made it back to Lombok, near Bali, more than two years later my sense of home, country and place in the world is still nowhere near being settled. Like most days, today before writing these pages I woke up to take my epileptic medication to stabilize myself. I sent my kids to school on another remote island in Indonesia before my mind shifted back to Ukraine, wondering how my sister in Kyiv is doing. If and when I have the energy and time, I scroll on Instagram to see what needs my attention and support on the ground there—even if I'm across the world in the middle of nowhere. Today, I donated to the family of an 18 year old Ukrainian sportsman who was killed last night on the streets in Germany for his support to Ukraine. In my feed I also saw pictures from an exhibition in Dubai where Russian 'businessmen' are selling sunflower oil sourced from the occupied city Melitopol, just 100 kilometers away from my hometown in Crimea. Don't they know that these are our lands, our sunflowers, and our products? It hurts me to see that, in Dubai, no one knew the difference. No one even seemed to care. But I do. And so does everyone in Melitopol, not to mention the countless other cities and villages in my homeland that have gone silent to the ears of the world.

I can't stop crying. Though I notice that my most recent tears taste different: they have lost the salt of their fear. What's left is a mix of dignity, will, love, and attempts at understanding. But, I still can't deny that it flows from a source of deep underlying shame.

I am desperate to map out a straightforward path to become a wise adult and to carve out a strong identity as a global citizen. I don't want any more years to pass where I feel this shame, to feel the regret that the evil has not stopped, to struggle to do my part when my reserves are empty. I don't want this weakened energy, trauma, and karma to pass on to my daughters. They have already absorbed too much. Somehow, I will find the path for us to move forward, to help rebuild what was lost within us, even if we never see our Ukrainian home that once was, again.

—

The past few years, if anything, have taught me that life does not move in a straight line, even though I desperately try to make it so. Life is dynamic and ever changing and mostly out of our control. Nevertheless, I now sense that I have incredible power to navigate through any path if I know how to focus and channel my energies. My situation has forced me to figure this situation out despite its difficulty. It is the hardest thing I have ever had to do.

As I write this my intuition is telling me to stop the doom scrolling, to take off my rose-colored glasses, to do my best to navigate the year ahead, and to envision how the next 5 to 10 years could play out if we could all just face the truth.

Beyond my personal situation—not to mention my fellow Ukrainians—the world is in a very dangerous place. Global warming, poly wars, technologies that are both used to kill and to heal, division and polarization, are now the realities of our everyday life.

Lines of real communication are broken, largely because of the misinformation and lies that we tell each other and ourselves. Beyond the farce of television and social media, which I won't even talk about here, we all avoid difficult conversations with our partners, colleagues, and friends. We skip visits to the dentist, we show up daily doing work that we dislike. And then we are shocked to receive unhappiness and weak immunity as a feedback from our body. So many people feel horrible, alone, and alienated, even if they have no direct exposure to the war(s) going on around the world. The lies everywhere in and around us create the vicious circle that connects our outer and inner worlds and vice versa.

I am ready to do my part to stop the lies, sensing deep into my own truth to let go of what no longer serves me, even when it hurts. I have experienced what it feels like to say goodbye to former partners and friends, who have escalated the war from the battlefields into the culture of our business and conversations.

I have discovered that life is very fragile, and I choose to devote mine to people who prioritize Truth and integrity over politics and power mongering. But, my Truth is not only about taking empowered action, it is about sensing Truth truthfully. My journey has shown me that we are ultimately information gathering organisms, what I call *Inforgs*, that generate meaning and truth from how we sense it through our conscience. It has been written about for a very long time, but our ability to differentiate fakes from truths is surely the 21st century skill that needs to be taught in every school. This is now beyond urgent. Only with our purified and attuned conscience can we meet others and fill our relationships with attention, empathy, and compassion.

Sincere human empathy and compassion are at the core of what makes us different from other species. These qualities are at the foundation of our humanity, the unique feelings we have that connect us to something bigger than ourselves. When I say "I'm here, what can I do for you?" I know that it is the most precious gift of life I can offer.

I have offered that a lot over the years, and learned to realize that there is also a catch. Just like the morbid airline safety instructions that tell us to cover ourselves first before helping those beside us, we need to provide empathy and love to ourselves before we can be of any use to others. For years, I've burned myself out so often working and volunteering days and nights out of my goodwill and over willingness to support, because I can and because I want to experience that connection of service. However, I have taken on too much and gone through mental illness as a result. I know now that I cannot offer help when I've lost connection with my own body and soul.

I think this is a lesson that applies to us all. In the blindness of offering unconditional support, there is a risk we become blind to not only ourselves, but to others around us too. In the end, no one walks away a winner—and we simply empower the realm of fakes and lies. It becomes a story of the blind leading the blind where no one knows where they are going. Maybe we humans should learn to trust our instincts more like animals do: Animals will never choose idiots to be their leaders!

My lingering feeling in this contemplation is that Love is not that romantic feeling I once thought it was. It is not about giving everything and letting things be as they are. When a mom does not let her child play late into the evening because she fears they will be tired, when the child is told not to touch anything that is hot, not to swim when it's windy, etc, she creates boundaries that limit the child's perception and direct experience of life. We must all learn first-hand how life works, how the law of cause and effect is built into everything. Love is leaning into this process, trusting that we will grow from our experiences and find the correct way to extract meaning from them.

The world has a problem with aggression, which is something very deep from our history and artificially created boundaries. The roots of this dig into the stories, the often subtle or outright lies, we tell ourselves and children. I remember once having coffee with another mom who was proudly sharing that she never buys books with bad characters in the story. "Yes, you can buy such a book" I said. But, unfortunately the world is not like that. When we create and accept false borders and boundaries, we sustain the realm of separation and lies that nourish the darkness, mental illness, and fear-based aggression that is now re-shaping our inner and outer landscapes. Love allows us to perceive the world the way it is and still be present, even when it is nothing close to romantic.

When I look back at myself two years ago, there is surely pain but no regrets. While the ongoing war has temporarily weakened me, I know it has made me wiser and more resilient. I am living through the difficulties of transforming my pain and suffering to wisdom and bolder dreams.

In my near future, I will walk into a new day, head to the construction site where we are building our new home in a tropical paradise; pick my kids from school that I co-founded; invite friends from all over the world to dinner; hug my parents before they go back to Ukraine. I am ready to contribute and serve in such a new way, which I hope will ripple out into the cosmos as a wish for new ways of living that lead to lasting peace through deeper connection.

My tears of shame will dry up, that I know. And I trust that my increasingly fearless heart will guide me to wisdom, even though I am a realist that knows the times ahead will still be difficult. I am ready to become the change I wish to see in the world, and invite you to do the same from wherever you are.

—

Liubov Shlapai *is a Social Entrepreneur*

Linda Lanzavecchia

There is no Finish Line to Cross

I recently found myself connecting the dots from childhood memories to recent years. The red string connecting all these dots, I believe, is nature. It was clearly during my childhood years that the seeds of my future passions started flourishing. I was lucky enough to experience at such a young age a life filled with adventures, wonders and explorations. I still struggle to remember moments of boredom. My most vivid memories are filled with hikes in the mountains with my grandpa, sailing in remote places around the world with my parents and, more recently, solo travels around the globe, driven by a deep curiosity to explore new places and a longing to understand myself better.

As I contemplate and attempt to articulate my current truth and the journey to this realisation, I am increasingly aware of the urgency of our environmental crisis. The trajectory of our planet's climate presents a daunting reality: By the time I'm 50, the world will not be a nice place to live in. Extreme weather events appear more often, heat waves increase in frequency and intensity, biodiversity loss is at unprecedented rates, sea levels rise and many other terrifying predictions yet to come. These wonders I used to play in as a child may, indeed, look very different in the near future. Unless, of course, we join forces to hinder this from happening.

It's a scary time to be a young adult in this era, confronted by the pressing challenges of our time. Yet, it's also an immensely captivating period to craft one's own narrative in the midst of this global transformation. My deep-rooted passion for nature, coupled with my ongoing journey of self-discovery and my education, unequivocally steer me towards contributing to the realm of climate change. I keenly feel the weight of my generation's duty to be the first to catalyse meaningful change and shoulder the responsibility of action. However, amidst this urgency, I can't shake the feeling of loneliness that accompanies the realisation that not everyone has taken the crucial step to grasp the importance of our collective efforts. This sense of solitude only reinforces my resolve to act.

The question that has guided my path until now is, "how can I be useful?" Discovering my passion for nature and the environment was my first step to finding the answer. As I started exploring the environmental space, I rapidly understood that climate change, and all other environmental issues, are simply symptoms of a greater dysfunction—the inability of humankind to protect our home and to live in a way that sustains future generations. As I delved deeper into "how can I be useful?" I felt an overwhelming pressure which evolved into a sense of constant frustration and a lack of trust in the world surrounding me. This 'climate anxiety' (a terrible name) manifested as a deep sense of loneliness. As well as a sense of not belonging, and not wanting to belong. I felt like a lonely island. And the more I exposed myself to climate news, research and studies, the more gloomy the future looked—mine as well as the one of my generation and the generations to come. Why were people not in the same state of panic as I was? Isn't keeping the planet alive and finding ways to make it thrive the only important thing right now? Not for the Earth itself—she would do well without us—but rather for humankind.

Eventually, I got tired of the feeling of being stuck in this problem. A series of things helped me overcome it. I started sharing my concerns with people I could relate to. A huge step was entering spaces where people shared my same concerns, such as my master's degree, or connecting to people who could inspire me, such as the Corporate Unplugged Forum friends. I learned small ways to make a difference and see small impacts. I allowed myself to get distracted with other things to get new oxygen and perspective. But what helped me most of all was my deliberate shift of attention to what I could influence—shifting from what is useful to what is meaningful to me, from what I can do for others, to understanding what I deeply care about. And as it turns out, this 'tiny' shift of perspective is helping me to be even more useful!

I am slowly realising that there may not be a solution to my question about my future. But, there might be a way around it!

Living in a hyperproductive society, it is easy to fall into the trap of hyper-perfectionism. We are trained to believe that having a big dream, and a clear vision, will make us achieve fulfillment and happiness. I thought that by picturing a 'perfect life' with a 'perfect job' and finding a valid aim, I could find my way towards achieving my life goals. But while focusing on future goals, events and achievements, life happens. Projecting myself in the future was making me forget to be truly present and confident. So I started taking tiny steps to actively dismantle my expectations of myself, and all the expectations that people around me projected on me. The immediate result? Relief!

The biggest teacher in this has certainly been my yoga journey. I ran into yoga thinking it would have fixed my anxiety and found a whole new realm to contemplate. Yoga taught me and is teaching me to stay in my discomfort and to accept without judging and labelling what I feel, think, and wish. And especially, that there is no ultimate state to achieve, but learning happens in the process. Finally, working with conscious embodied practices slowly opens up space for more awareness. I do realise that I'm more aware of myself, of my surroundings, of the effects of my actions and many other complicated connections that happen every minute.

I'm still at the very beginning of this whole process. I have no idea where this will lead. But for now, I'm pondering my biggest learning: That there might be absolutely no sense in having a life aim. Does my insight come from a place of total confusion? Or perhaps it is actually true that in life there is no finish line to cross. Rather a natural and infinite sequence of experiences, learnings and moments that continuously unfold—like waves in the blue ocean. All I can do is to have patience, appreciate the process and remain curious throughout all of it.

This does not mean not having a purpose. Purpose is essential to guide the path. I simply believe that being focused on one thing, having one single picture in mind, might exclude an infinite number of marvellous, fascinating possibilities and solutions. So I'm changing my paradigm from aiming for a useful job and a useful life to simply live a life that I believe is meaningful, and live it every single day with pure curiosity, without expecting any prize at the end.

As I reflect on my journey and share these thoughts with you, I find myself looking forward with a sense of optimism and purpose. What I long for is a future where awareness becomes the cornerstone of our existence—where every action we take is embedded with a deep understanding of its impact on the environment, on society, and on the intricate web of life that sustains us all. I dream of a world where humans live in harmony with nature, recognising ourselves not as separate entities, but as integral parts of a greater whole. In this future, intergenerational experiences flourish, where we embrace the wisdom of our elders while fostering an environment where children's innate curiosity and wonder are nurtured. Together, we learn and grow, drawing inspiration from each other and from the natural world that surrounds us. Together means more than just collective action; it means sharing knowledge, experiences, and perspectives.

My friends in the Corporate Unplugged Forum are not only a source of inspiration but also teachers, showing me the importance of togetherness in tackling the challenges we face. They remind me that true progress is made when we collaborate, learn from each other, and lift each other up. It's a vision of interconnectedness, where every choice we make is guided by a reverence for life and a commitment to leave the world better than we found it. As I embark on this journey, I do so with hope in my heart, knowing that together, we can create a future that is not only sustainable but also filled with beauty, meaning, and possibility.

I realise that my mini-essay—like my life—is a work in progress. Hopefully, I will discover more truths on my journey through a life well lived. But for now, I've shared with you what life is from the perspective of my 25-year-old self :) To be continued. Love and light to you dear reader, whoever you are. Namaste.

—

Linda Lanzavecchia *is an Architect and Environmental and Climate Advisor*

Lisen Schultz

Our Dependence on All Life

My seven-year-old hands examine the construction of the feather I've found in my granny's old barn. Separating the thin barbs from one another, noticing how they cling together and then let go when I insist. A sensation of release as I slowly move down the feather, barb after barb. "When I was a child I would try to heal the feathers instead," I hear my granny observe softly. I hadn't noticed her coming and I blush as I realize she is not happy with what I'm doing. I try to bring the barbs back together again, but the tiny hooks won't connect.

Decades later, tears stream down the cheeks of my seven-year-old daughter as I meet her after school. Some boys have poked an anthill during recess and she just can't understand how anyone can be so cruel. "I tried to tell them that this is the ants' home that they have worked really hard to build, and I even asked them how they would feel if a giant ant came to destroy their house. But they just laughed and kept going." The teachers hadn't intervened even when she asked them for help, and my daughter is devastated. My heart hurts for her and the world she has to grow up in. But her attention to the ants' perspective and rights fills me with gratitude.

—

For a scientist, holding something to be true is difficult. The continuous questioning is a fundamental part of my being in the world, and with every attempt at putting a truth into words, there is a counter-truth asking for attention. But there is one realization about the human condition that I do hold to be true, right now: All humans depend on the larger web of life to survive and thrive, the biosphere. And, if we give equal weight to care and curiosity as we engage in the world, the biosphere can hold us for many generations to come. As with all truths, my realization comes from a combination of experience, reflection and learning from people I trust. Including my granny, my daughter, and scholars in my field.

My granny Frideborg lived alone in the countryside, where she enjoyed her own company and was surrounded by non-human friends: The white wagtail Nikodemus who came for breakfast every morning, a moose she often met in the forest, and even the rat Flora, who lived in her house and was fed in the living room. A lot of granny's food came from the forest and her freezer was filled to the brim with blue berries and mushrooms. My favorite book in her library was an alpine flora with color photographs of the most beautiful flowers growing in the mountains of Austria and Switzerland. She would read to me about the fascinating features that helped them survive the harsh conditions of wind, snow and drought. How they would stay close to the ground, develop tiny hairs and thick leaves for protection, and strong colors to attract pollinators during their short season of blossoming. How their delicate, flexible stems would bend in the wind instead of breaking. With granny, life was to be respected, admired, and cared for, but also to be explored and enjoyed, be it through foraging in the forest, making music together or carefully examining feathers. When she passed away just before my 11th Christmas, she left me with an ethical compass that has guided me ever since.

A few years after her passing, I had my first experience of not being able to follow that compass, no matter how hard I tried. In school, we learned that the gas in our hairspray bottles ripped a hole in the protective ozone layer, that rainforest was being cut down to make our furniture, and that factories and cars polluted the air and the water that all living creatures depend on. Somehow, we were destroying life simply by living. In response, I would turn off the lights at home, shorten my showers, nag on my parents and siblings to recycle whatever could be recycled. I even thought of not having children, or maybe not growing up at all, to minimize my burden on the planet. But to this last thought, my inner lust for life objected. It told me that human life also should have a place. I realized that I really wanted humans to be around on this planet, to make music and art, to enjoy all the beauty that this part of the universe holds, and to turn things right. And so I decided to dedicate my time to exploring how humans could find a more mutual relationship with life.

At the university, I studied biology and geology, as I figured I needed to learn as much as I could about life if I wanted to find ways of reconnecting with it. The class room was filled with nature-lovers, and we spent many weeks in the field, learning about everything from microbes to mammals and the ecosystems that connect them all, the evolution of life, the history of planet Earth and its eternal cycles of air, water, minerals, and energy. My fascination and love for life in all its forms grew, as did my scientific knowledge, but the role of people in all of this remained hidden in the fields of natural science that I engaged with. (On a side note, science is in many ways the ultimate pursuit of human curiosity, but it is not always combined with care. I met a professor in biology once who had specialized in a certain species of spiders, because he was so fascinated by them. His curiosity about their life history and role in the larger ecosystem led him to remove all spiders he could find on a few islands and study the effects. He described how it had taken him and several assistants all summer to succeed with the extinction mission, and then he spent years following and analyzing the response of the island ecosystems. Whether the professor's favorite spider species recovered on the islands or not remains unclear, but the study found that in their absence other species took their place in the food chain.)

It was not until I took a course at the Department of Systems Ecology that people came back into the picture. Here, Carl Folke, a professor of ecological economics, explained how humans are shaping the biosphere, from local farms to global water flows, but also how we can rediscover our dependence on nature, and become wiser stewards of the ecosystems. He talked about the need to bring together knowledge from indigenous communities and scientific communities to find ways forward, and the need to bring ecology into decision-making, in policy as well as in business. He also opened the door for me to pursue a PhD within the UN programme Millennium Ecosystem Assessment, where I became one of 1,500 experts tasked with assessing the status of the world's ecosystems and the benefits they provide to people, and building human capacity to manage them better for the future. We found, as many others have before and after, that the planet is losing species and ecosystems at an alarming rate, and that this loss is harming people. But, we also found many examples of practices and policies that help people meet their needs in collaboration with nature, rather than through exploitation.

During my lifetime, scientists have concluded that humanity has become a force of change on the planet on par with geological forces. Some suggest that we have entered the age of humans, the Anthropocene, where the very stability of the climate that allowed for our civilizations to emerge is under threat. Others argue that it is not humanity as a whole that caused the Anthropocene, but particular ways of life in particular parts of the world. Nevertheless, the conditions for life on this planet are now shaped by our burning of fossil fuels, conversion of forests and grasslands into cropland, construction of new chemicals, roads and buildings, and extraction of timber, fish and metals. One could argue that this development is a result of unlimited curiosity and exploration of new technologies and terrain, or that it's driven by care for ourselves as humans and a strong desire to meet human needs and aspirations. In any case, I believe there is a missing piece that allows us to mentally disconnect from the web of life. Curiosity without care seems to result in cruelty. And care without curiosity is easily misdirected.

So what makes me believe that the biosphere can hold space for humanity into the future? If I am really honest, I believe it because I want it to become true. It is a leap of faith, but I think it is the best bet we have, to believe that it is possible, and to search for paths that lead us there. There are many science-based scenarios that show how such a future could unfold, concluding that there is enough for all of us on this beautiful planet, as long as we leave the fossil fuel-driven, linear economy behind, and develop more sophisticated ways of collaborating with each other and nature. But, what really fuels my conviction is when I see people put their hearts, minds and hands into making the future happen. And at the core of it all, I sense a love for life, and the care and curiosity that comes with it.

—

My daughter Nova, youngest in our family of six children, is now a teenager and she still loves all animals (including ticks and mosquitoes, who are not to be killed in her presence, only carefully removed if they bite). For her fifth birthday, she wrote the names of three poisonous snakes at the top of her wish list and in spite of my resistance, she continued asking for a snake pet until she turned thirteen. By then, she had convinced me that she was ready for the responsibility and so I helped her realize her dream. The garter snake Doris has lived with us ever since, and she has even won my heart with her beautiful colors, fascinating movements and positive effect on Nova's mood.

Together with my granny, my daughter and the many generations to come, I wish for all humans to revitalize their relationships with the biosphere. As individuals, organizations, communities and nations, we can rediscover our dependence on life, in all its enchanting (and repulsive) forms. And then, we can turn our curiosity towards caring for the spiders, reptiles, plants, and humans that make up our only home in the universe. Carefully connecting the barbs of a feather, once parted by a curious child.

—

Lisen Schultz *is Associate Professor in Sustainability Science, Deputy Director for the Stockholm Resilience Center, Stockholm University, Director of Education and the Programme Director for the center's executive programme in resilience thinking.*

Mario Solari

Reflecting on Heroes

Heroes show us not the path to our own happiness, but the path to our own selves—George Bernard Shaw

In the quiet moments between the relentless ticking of the clock and the ceaseless demands of daily life, I have often found myself captured by a singular, introspective query: *Have I, in certain chapters of my life, drifted away from my true essence? And do I really understand what my true essence is?* These are not questions born of fleeting curiosity, but rather a profound inquiry into the human condition, a reflection on whether this sense of disconnection from our core selves is a universal experience, inevitable and woven into the fabric of the life system we are immersed in.

Three years ago, this existential query transformed from a general pondering into a deeply personal crisis. On paper, my life read like a story of success and fulfilment: an honourable career as a professional investor and partner in a prestigious investment firm, a beautiful family with a loving wife and three daughters, a circle of friends, the luxury of time, and a passion for trail ultra-running that kept me physically and spiritually grounded. Yet, beneath this facade, a storm was brewing—a storm of confusion and instability. My energy drifted away from the job I so passionately loved for many years, and I couldn't understand why.

The journey through this storm was not one I undertook alone. My wife, a beacon of wisdom and my companion since our youth, stood steadfastly by my side. Her insights, coupled with our shared adventures in self-exploration and into the philosophies of life—as well as many hours spent on the trails, meditation, yoga, books and podcasts—became my compass. Coincidentally, her academic engagement with the studies of happiness under the tutelage of Professor Tal Ben-Shahar provided serendipitous guidance.

This period of introspection led me to a revelation, both simple and profound: The architecture of human society, with its complex social structures and expectations, almost guarantees a departure from our true essence as individuals on this planet. This divergence often manifests in various forms of discomfort—a pervasive dissatisfaction, a waning of motivation, or even physical and mental afflictions such as anxiety and depression. It's as though the societal matrix into which we are pressed shapes us in ways that obscure our true selves.

Amidst this realization, I grappled with a haunting question: As my life nears its end (hopefully many decades from now), how will I judge its value? How closely aligned is my life with those fundamental principles and values that resonate at the very core of my being? This query lingered, challenging me to confront and reconcile my lived experiences with my innermost convictions.

But before I could tackle this existential question, was there a way I could confidently define my true essence, my life's purpose?

In seeking answers, I discovered that each of us harbours a set of core values and principles that define who we are at our deepest level. These essential truths vary widely among individuals— some are driven by a compulsion to create, to bring new ideas and paradigms into existence; others find their calling in service to those in need, dedicating their lives to the upliftment of the marginalized and suffering. And there are those who feel most alive when immersed in the natural world, bearing a profound connection to the earth and an intense desire to protect and preserve it. But it also became evident that as we grow, our awareness of societal norms and the pressure to belong often lead us to suppress or alter our natural tendencies. Societal influence can catalyse a departure from our true essence, prompting us to make decisions that, over time, steer us further from our core selves.

Sensing that my professional life may have disconnected from my true essence, the quest to uncover my core being became imperative. This journey, however, presented its own set of challenges. How does one begin to peel back the layers of societal conditioning, personal doubts, and the myriad influences that shape our paths?

Taking on the quest of uncovering my own essence led me back to the innocence of childhood, a time before the intrusion of societal expectations and stereotypes. I tried to dig deep and bring back as many memories from when I was perhaps between seven and twelve years old. I asked my parents about the tendencies they saw most clearly in me as their eldest child. I contemplated the purity of my younger self's interests and inclinations, untainted by the desire to conform.

The answer, however—or at least a part of it—came from an

unexpected direction: the stories and lives of those we admire most deeply, our *heroes,* those individuals whose impact and influence on you has been profound and transformative. These heroes, I learned, serve as mirrors to our souls, reflecting the virtues, aspirations, and core values that we hold dear, perhaps even subconsciously. By examining the qualities in them that we admire, we gain insights into our own essence and what truly moves us. This process of reflection is not just an exercise in admiration but a deep, introspective journey into understanding the fibres of our own being.

In this light, the image of my grandfather, Dante, took on new significance. His life was not just a series of accomplishments but a testament to living one's values in the purest form. Dante was born into modest beginnings, his family having emigrated from Italy to Chile during the Second World War, in search of a better future. Despite the challenges of adapting to a new country, Dante's early life was marked by a strong work ethic and a commitment to education, values instilled by his parents. His dual role as a student and a contributor to his family's humble grocery store did not deter him from excelling academically and athletically.

But Dante's true legacy, the essence of his being, was his unwavering dedication to his three greatest passions: his family, nature, and helping the underprivileged. His academic pursuits in agronomy and his significant contributions to Chile's agricultural knowledge base were driven by a profound love for and connection with the natural world. This love was not confined to the realm of academia; it was a lived experience, deeply intertwined with his personal life as he spent most of his later years immersed in the mountains.

Serving for over two decades as mayor and councillor of Lo Prado, one of Santiago's poorest municipalities, Dante's impact was transformative. His tenure was not defined by mere administrative successes but by a genuine, heartfelt commitment to improving the lives of the community's residents. His efforts were often quiet and unheralded, focusing on individual needs with a generosity and dedication that were both personal and profound. Dante's legacy, as revealed in the outpouring of respect and love at his funeral, saw hundreds of people who showed up totally unexpectedly, reflecting his essence: a man who lived for others through a deep commitment to public service, which included secretly giving most of his wealth away to help many individuals in need.

Reflecting on my grandfather's life and the values he embodied offered me a clearer understanding of my own essence. I was fortunate to spend most of my formative years very close to him, observing him and learning from his example. His dedication to family, nature, and to those most in need always resonated with me on a deep level, highlighting my own inclinations.

The memory of my grandfather helped me find a path to a better understanding of my innermost motivations – through the many layers that life had laid on top—and inspired me to take a course of greater alignment with those core motivations and values.

The process of realigning my professional life to better reflect my true essence hasn't been straightforward and is probably never totally complete. It requires a willingness to question deeply ingrained aspects of my identity and to confront the discomfort of change. Yet, I am grateful that I found the courage to make a difficult, non-obvious professional pivot, trusting that a life lived in harmony with my core values would ultimately be more fulfilling and meaningful.

In sharing this, I do so with the hope that it might offer a gentle nudge for others to consider their own heroes and what those figures reflect about their deepest values and aspirations. The journey to align one's life with their true essence is deeply personal and unique to each of us. My grandfather's story is a beacon for me, illuminating a path of love, dedication, and service. It serves not as a directive, but as a humble example of the richness that comes from living in harmony with one's core values.

This realization has been a guiding light for me, and perhaps, in sharing this, it might light the way for others on their own path to authenticity.

—

Mario Solari *is an Investor and Ultra-Trail runner.*

Jayce Pei Yu Lee

Love **in the Twists and Turns**

For the past five years I have travelled frequently from my home in Taipei to different countries. Somehow, amidst this constant movement, I have felt a sense of being lost, unsure of where I truly belonged and how enduring this transient lifestyle would be. It was during this period that I made a New Year's resolution: to write something every day, capturing a moment that resonated with me through writing. I was inspired by one of my dear colleagues and artist friends, Alfredo Carlo. This practice became a means for me to reflect on my identity and inner thoughts, engaging in a dialogue with myself.

Through this process, I unexpectedly discovered something profound within myself. I realized that the discipline cultivated over the years served as a prelude to what was to unfold. In 2022, I embarked on the Mosaic 365 project, a creative endeavor to create one drawing a day, without pre-planning and no theme in advance, allowing creation to flow spontaneously from within. This has become a steadfast creative salvation for me. Whenever faced with difficulties in life, I have found solace in recalling moments where I sat at my desk, pen and markers in hand, and poured my thoughts onto paper or on my iPad. In those instances, the act of creating instilled within me a sense of courage, reinforcing my belief that I could overcome any challenges I encountered.

Somehow, this has became a healing process for me to connect with my inner self. Through steady writing, making and creating, I uncovered something true emanating from within, enabling me to witness, embrace who I am, and ultimately let go of the old self, moving onward. This echoed in me the wisdom of Robert Frost: "Poetry is what gets lost in translation."

Life is a mystery that words or essays often cannot fully describe, capturing the beauty and awe within it. However, through the lines of poetry, seemingly broken, inconsistent, and odd phrases come to life, creating a sense of rhythm that mirrors human heartbeats, echoing the creative muse, and resonating with my own artistic expression. This expression is filled with my passions, curiosities, and dedication, drawing from the depths of my being.

The truth I am holding now is quietly settling within the inner meadow of my being. A vast mosaic landscape pieced together by seasons of change. Pearls rise without leaving a trace, only to disappear beneath the summer gaze.

—

Love in the Twists and Turns

Sometimes,
what we pursue throughout our lives
isn't necessarily
the things that are obvious.
Instead, it's
the true selves
hidden somewhere
in the mirror of reality.
In the process of stepping into the unknown,
we shouldn't only focus on
the primal desires and cravings,
but also maintain curiosity and openness
towards the delicate possibilities
lingering on the edge.
Because with a moment of distraction,
we may miss the destined beauty
brushing past us.

Pearl Rising

The land, the air, the sky,
all enveloped in a curtain of darkness,
engulfed the sight and the conscience,
like the rumbling of vice and abyss.
Never fade, my rising pearl,
go break through the clouds,
forever shines never in silence,
and glows wildly with mad existence.

Change

To be the change from within,
living on the land of possibilities,
the road is sometimes lonely,
and less traveled with uncertainty.

Follow the invisible rays of arrows,
and the magnificent Mekong river flow.
You don't know what you don't know,
just listen with soft pause:
be steady, and go slow.

Summer Gaze
The heatwaves,
stayed above the tips of chartreuse green,
mixed with the light touch of summer breeze.
I say: born free, flee and be the ultimate escapee,
never turning back, farewell to all these
years of summer gaze.

Love in the Twists and Turns *(in traditional Chinese)*
愛在迂迴曲折處

有時候
我們一生在追尋的
並不是哪些
顯而易見的東西。

反而是
隱藏在某處
真實鏡裡的自己。

在踏入未知的過程中
不單單只專注在
原始的渴望與慾望
對於駐足於邊緣的微妙可能
也得保持好奇與開放

因為 稍一閃神
便與註定的美好
擦身而過。

Jayce Pei Yu Lee *is a Visual catalyst and graphic facilitator based in Taipei, Taiwan. She is an artist, a scribe and a maverick storyteller. She is a core team member of The Value Web and of The Presencing Institute led by MIT professor Otto Scharmer. She also drives the visual practice movement in the Asia Pacific region.*

Laura Inserra

The **Essence of the Universe is Vibration**

If you want to find the secrets of the universe, think in terms of energy, frequency and vibration—Nikola Tesla

A ray of truth I carry in my heart is that music is one of the most powerful tools to experience the vibrational nature of existence.

Since I was a child I was enchanted by the 'invisible world', and music was one of the easiest ways to tap into it. It has taken me decades of cross-cultural studies in various schools of wisdom, scientific research, and spiritual pathways to prove that truth to myself and to others. Nowadays, I live and create within that truth. How did I get here? Let's take a moment to go back in time, and travel through space…

It was the mid-seventies when I was born in Sicily, a powerful island in southern Italy, with the most active stratovolcano in the world, Mount Etna. I grew up in a town called Lentini, and a tiny seaside village facing the Mediterranean Sea called Baia del Silenzio, which literally means Bay of Silence. I was deeply in touch with nature, but also living in a very narrow-minded culture and intense environment. Those were times marked by mistreatment of women, heavy political corruption, and the Mafia being at the peak of its bloody power.

We couldn't afford to have many toys, but Sicilian is a very animistic language, so I was playing with nature. I was talking to the sea, the moon, plants, stones, or even objects, as if the world around me was alive. I could say I was living a shamanic life, meaning a reality where everything was sensorial, and had a unique energetic quality, a certain personality. I was connected to the natural world in a visceral way. Maybe I was born that way, or perhaps it was only in nature that I could feel safe and connected.

From where we lived we could see the volcano. When it was erupting, my grandmother would often point at it and ask "u senti?" In Sicilian, as well as in Italian, the verb 'sentire' means to hear, but the same verb also means to feel. Because of the distance, I couldn't hear the volcano rumbling. But, I could feel its energy in my bones, in my skin, in my emotions. The thunderous voice of its activity. Mineral scents of ash floating in the air like fireflies at night. The light blue color of the sky soaked with reds, yellows, and oranges. Molten fiery lava flowing as liquid gold all along its hips. An ancient feeling of reverence for the supreme Mother Nature.

Sicilian is also a language that has no future tense. Basically we refer to the future using the present tense, as if it's happening now! Grandma was often saying "today we are here, tomorrow, we don't know. So, let's play." This gave me an innate awareness of presence, and a sense of the ephemeral nature of life. Everyday I felt it could have been my last one on this planet.

At a very young age I had my first mystical sound experience with my brother's guitar. One day, while he was gone, I went to his room, I placed the guitar on his bed, and I started to tap with a pen on top of the open strings. Imagine all those acoustic vibrations and harmonics floating in the room… It was magical. I felt transported to another dimension, an invisible world I always felt around me, especially when in nature. But, now I could tap into it through music.

Since that moment, I started tapping on every surface and playing as many instruments as you can imagine. Having a great sense of rhythm, the djembe, the tammorra, or any hand percussion were my favorites. I could improvise with a bass guitar, a saxophone, flutes, or just using my voice. Pretty soon music became a shelter for me, a way to calm down my inner and outer environment, a place where I could rearrange chaos into order, create harmony and experience it with others.

It was the beginning of the eighties when one day my uncle came back home with a Commodore 64, one of the earliest home computers in history. Passionate about technology, he taught me how to plug in the keyboard to my grandmother's television and program video games. Now I could make my own animated virtual games by tapping on a plastic keyboard. I felt I was creating magic! So in parallel to nature and music, I developed a passion for technology and its potential.

All along I had many big questions I needed answers for. Where do we come from? Why are we here? Where did grandma go when she died? I often spent my evenings with my older sister's artist friends, mostly in their 30s and 40s, gathering in one of their homes after dinner, sharing art, viewing slides, and jamming with whatever instruments or objects were at hand.

One of them, Pippo Pagano, was into esoteric books and willing to share his knowledge and music with me. He right away recognized my inner call and gifts. I spent most of my teens with him, playing, debating, and pontificating about life. I started to study alchemy, learn about eastern philosophies, and do energetic practices of all kinds. I had such a profound desire to experience the fullness of life and its magic before it was my turn to 'check out'.

I moved to Rome to study psychology, ethnomusicology, and dig more into spiritual practices. I started to teach percussion, improvisation, didgeridoo and circular breathing. I never had a teacher but I had the ability to share what I had learned as a self-taught musician. The students loved my teachings, mostly based on expressing themselves through their instruments in a simple, instinctive, and practical way.

Combining my musical and technological skills, I started to make soundtracks for movies, theater, and dance companies. Music became a way to transcend reality, evoke emotions, and describe the unseen world. I had many students and they were becoming very good. I felt it was time for me to deepen my musical study, and have a more formal education.

I entered the Conservatorium and studied classical percussion. I was fascinated by how most musicians were able to play very complex scores by reading sheet music. At the same time I was shocked they were not able to improvise, or to simply express themselves with their instruments. It felt very sad and inconceivable for me. As if they were trapped in their technical and intellectual understanding of music. Plus most of them were frustrated with their instrument, and the fact that thousands of other musicians played those classical compositions way way better than they did.

I was already passionate about producing cross-disciplinary events, and blurring the boundaries between performers and audience when, in 2003, I was invited to Burning Man in

Nevada's Black Rock Desert. I was in awe, witnessing how art, nature, and community can impact people. A few years later I moved to the San Francisco Bay Area to be closer to my ex-partner, and to learn more about cutting edge technologies.

For years I kept studying and practicing with gurus, healers, and shamans from all over the world. What I noticed was common in each one of these traditions and religions, was that at the 'beginning' there was a sound, a vibrational essence, from which the Universe was born. In the Bible, for example, we read "God said, let there be light, and there was light." Most people believe that at the beginning there was light, but actually God 'said' let there be light, therefore first He vocalized His intention, and then boom… light there was. In Vedic philosophy, sound is believed to be the essence of the Universe, *Nāda Brahma*, which literally means Brahma, the Creator, is Nāda, primordial sound. The Hopi traditions tell the story of the 'Spider Grandmother'. She crafted the humans out of clay, and gave life to those inanimate forms by singing the Song of Creation over them. Science talks about the 'beginning' as a Big Bang. What is that if not a huge sound? It was pretty clear to me that what we call 'sound' was a powerful metaphor to grasp the essence of the Universe.

I founded a multidisciplinary performing arts non-profit organization, focused on creating immersive and participatory art productions in a variety of natural sites and man-made environments. One of my brainchildren was the annual Art in Nature Festival, featuring hundreds of artists performing along the one mile Redwood Regional Park Stream Trial, in Oakland. I wanted people to experience that art is the expression of a creative force we all have inside, and that nature is the greatest artist and teacher of all.

I deepened my explorations around the Mongolian shamanic tradition and the use of drumming and chanting to induce trance. For millennia, our ancestors have used music to create sacred ceremonies, to be in symbiosis with nature, to transit to different states of consciousness, to predict events, to mourn, to grieve, and to heal. In the sacred instruments they were making, there was a certain signature, a certain quality of energy that could amplify our human ability to connect, to evolve, and to access our inner guidance and healing.

I couldn't find a lot of 'colleagues' with whom to share notes, plus our modern society was giving almost zero value to those understandings. It was a pretty solo journey with a lot of challenges along the path. I was too visionary, not willing to make many compromises, and not able to fit in one specific category or social label.

With much courage and determination, I put into my work all the fruits of my personal and professional development. I called myself a sound alchemist and my work MetaMusic. I was using music less as entertainment and more as a form of entrainment. Those who were exposed to my work were having profound breakthroughs, shifts of consciousness, out of body experiences, deep inner transformations, and all kinds of physical, emotional, and mental healing.

I became more and more well known for the uniqueness of my style and the rarity of my instruments. I was invited to remarkable conferences, leadership retreats, and gatherings, till one day I was approached by a Bay Area entrepreneur who asked me "How can we scale your work?" That was a pretty weird question, I thought. What does it mean? Removing me from the equation and reproducing my music via computers? Well... I took it as an exciting challenge, and a possibility to make my work accessible to the world at large.

As a good alchemist, I put all my gifts together and refined my ways to use technology to scale my work without losing its integrity. It was 2018 when I premiered what I call Chambers of AWE, immersive and transformative sound journeys made with ceremonial instruments, field recordings, and cutting edge technology.

Through technology I was able to amplify some of those sources of sound, reveal some of their inaudible frequencies, and augment their properties. Then I infused these productions with what I learned from my teachers and the whole gamut of my experiences, including the direct observation of nature. In these environments, these chambers, music becomes experiential. You feel the music with your whole body. You become music. Why? Because you are sound!

Your body is resonating, your cells are vibrating, your heart is drumming... You are an orchestra. When you are exposed to sound, by sympathetic resonance, your cells start to oscillate widely. In that movement, energy is released. Today we know that energy carries information, so during these music experiences you might release obstructive emotions, expand your sense of self, access ancient memories or future visions, and much more. And because you are sound, the more you are exposed to ancient sounds and sacred environments, the more you can tap into the sacred and profound experience of being human.

The impact of these productions was beyond any expectation. I envisioned using dome-like structures and to build multiple physical Chambers of AWE around the world. I got my first commission and boom... the pandemic hit! From in-person gatherings, I transitioned my work to mainly live-streams, reaching people from diverse cultures and backgrounds around the world. Getting global feedback made me realize that what I was able to offer was way more profound and needed than I could have ever imagined.

Witnessing the global challenges of our modern times, and the suffering we inflict on nature and each other, I felt the duty and responsibility to share my gifts widely. I believed that having a certain mystical or spiritual sensibility would make us better humans.

I started a guided sound journeys series called Shelter in Music, helping people cope with the pandemic, mourn their losses, connect to their inner guidance, and access their innate capacity to heal. During these weekly livestreams I invited people to set an intention, close their eyes, and allow music to show them where they need to go, what they need to feel, to hear, to envision, to heal. The segregated walls of the confinement were disappearing and the sense of time and space expanded infinitely, allowing us to become one collective body. How was that possible?

In ancient schools of wisdom it was known that humans are electromagnetic transmitters who send out thoughts and emotions, and have a corresponding attraction to what we have sent out. Basically we become a tuning fork that can tune 'energy' to a specific 'frequency' and have a tangible effect on 'reality'. Music is able to orchestrate scattered vibrations in an harmonious order, creating organized energetic 'forms' of e-motions (energy in motion). Our body is also energy in motion, and can project energy into thought-forms. When we visualize an outcome, through our intent, we are investing mental and physical energy into these thought-forms. By feeling the outcome in our whole body as if it had already happened, we are investing augmented energy into potential 'forms' of manifestation. In other words, when we focus our intention and our feelings to envision an outcome, we make a 'silent' action that creates a tangible impact in our inner and outer environment. That's one of many ways to look at it.

Let me take us back here, where I am right now, while playing with words for a piece of writing. Today, I live in an enchanted chalet in the Berkeley Hills, overlooking the Bay's body of water and the Golden Gate Bridge. My backyard is Tilden Park, where I went for a hike just a few minutes ago. I feel rooted in my life-path and work like a mother tree. More than talking about the vibrational essence of the Universe, I am passionate about creating occasions for people to experience that truth within themselves.

I found my own way to scale the impact of my work by founding Chambers of AWE LLC, a mission-based multimedia production company, creating immersive and transformative experiences in planetariums and similar venues. Our productions feature musical journeys crafted with ceremonial instruments and field-recordings, enhanced with 360° visuals and AI-generated content rooted in ancient wisdom. These 'chambers' facilitate experiences that open consciousness to deep feelings of wonder, make us experience the luminous essence of being human, and create a felt connection to the visible and invisible world.

No matter where in the world our feet are touching the ground, we are all interconnected and living in symbiosis on this divine planet. More than ever, I feel it is time to be creative together, united with each other and with nature. We could make great use of music and ancient practices to send harmonized energy to ourselves and to all forms of life on our planet, envisioning a more regenerative and healing living.

Why don't we do it now for a minute. Take a long breath… and slowly breathe out any tension in your body. Take another deep one… hold it for a second… and slowly exhale any tension in your emotions. Take another long one… and with the exhale, let go of any mental process.

Now you will take a few minutes on your own. You will close your eyes. Envision a benevolent outcome you want to see manifested for yourself and for all beings. Breathe that vision into your heart. Feel it in your whole body as it is already happening. And exhale it into the entire Universe as pure, vibrating golden light.

I'll meet you there...

—

Laura Inserra *is a sound alchemist, educator, multi-instrumentalist, public speaker, multimedia producer.*

Jan Broman

The **Builder**

I build places. Places where people meet. Where they are woken up by an unexpected impression, into a realm out of the ordinary. I have seen it so many times, how extraordinary art or music sparks something new inside a person. As if they suddenly realize an aspect of themselves they did not know they had. It takes them to new levels. It makes them grow and talk to each other. Real change is created in the interaction between people. I want to initiate conversations that truly matter, to help people reflect together through a lens that is fresh and rejuvenating.

I started out as a photographer, taking pictures to cover news stories. Soon I realized that pictures are themselves the best storytellers. Something powerful and real happens between a good picture and the observer. An imprint that lives on long after the experience. But we need places and spaces where this can happen.

Where you meet yourself, each other and the world. I soon realized this was the kind of place I was here to create, and started by building a space for Photography. I called it Fotografiska.

From the start, I knew that it would be so much more than a museum. A community of sorts with a club, culinary experiences, a curated shop and education through a photography school. A genuine hotspot for interaction. Our project had growth programmed into it and soon scaled from Stockholm to Tallinn and New York. It was a dream that came true, but at the same time it turned out totally different than I had expected—as projects always do. Good projects carry their own creative power that drives them forward. As founders, we need to know when to let go.

I am happy to have my experience. I have learnt to hand over to others what I do not excel in but they do. Fotografiska taught me *not* to involve myself in every detail, so that people would not look to me for every decision instead of bringing their own competency forward. I now have the courage to trust the organization and let the best idea win. I am the founder, the keeper of the mission and the vision. My role is to inspire, make us walk that extra mile, understand that we are creating something bigger than ourselves.

The places we are building now are grander. They have to be, it does not make sense to do something less challenging than what you did before. I want to build places that are bigger than the art inside and universal enough to scale to other cities and cultures. I have lost count of the projects I started, but I always come back to that same theme. Creating places for meaningful connections, where the meaning and the spark comes from art, music—and that certain quality that is the trademark of true creativity.

When embarking on a new project, I am always pulled in by the thought that something needs to exist that was not there before.

I know it can be done and that it needs to be done. It is a source of energy to me, the friction between how it is and how it could be. But I never know how it will turn out until it is finished. Or at least ready to share, in my world things are never quite done. This is what life seems to have in mind for me, and I am happy to follow the lead. There is nothing more meaningful to me.

What signifies a good photographer from the rest is composition. And the ability to see where there is a picture to be captured. Where there are enough elements that can be brought to work together. The same thing goes for an entrepreneur creating experiences. You need to make sure that the guests are included in all the layers of hospitality that build the experience. And have the courage to let the experience be open, let go of controlling the content and instead focus on the operational side.

All the components must be geared up to 100%, then brought to work together. From the welcoming at the entrance, the atmosphere in the restaurant, bar and shops, to the design of the amenities. From the flow in buying tickets to the uniqueness of the exhibition. You need to be the composer who keeps the vision intact in every single detail of the project. But, there is no use solving problems before they arise. Instead, use speed and a problem solving mentality to handle challenges as they arise.

Generally, people seem to settle for too little too early. The itching feeling that something could be done even better drives me and everyone on the team. We are never quite ready, but build into the business model and our culture that nothing can ever remain static. We need to constantly grow with our mission.

When you create something new that has not been done before, recruiting is everything. Find competent people who excel in their specific part. Who keeps pushing every detail towards perfection. Then give them space to make the decisions in their own turf. Gain speed and precision by reducing the number of people who have a say in each part. And make sure the vision is guiding every step.

Mediocrity is the pitfall, general consensus and compromises will certainly lead you there. You could never come up with something new if you try to improve what others are already doing. Don't take yourself so seriously, have a good laugh and let humor bring you to the verge of foolishness. That is where you find the greatest ideas.

People rarely believe in my ideas, they do not think people will come. But what they miss is that I build on the force of attraction. Our crowd helps us create the identity of the place and build the brand that reflects how we sound, look and feel. What our values are. The brand gives us the layers that we fill with content. In a place where people like to hang out, we become a trusted source, a home. In a way it is all about hospitality, being welcoming and having good intentions. We cannot change people, but we can invite them to be more of themselves— by giving knowledge in new ways. Facts become boring on their own; but, when combined with entertainment you get groundbreaking content with something to say. Being boring is failure to me. Success is the opposite—an out of the world experience that gives life to important questions inside you.

Historically, truth has been bent and distorted by those with the power to spread their words. But now, the truth is up for grabs to anyone who creates a channel. Algorithms make cells of opinions that are not questioned, where perspectives get distorted. The world needs better reflections of truth. Our lack of it threatens democracy.

Even in Scandinavia we wrestle with the democratic paradox— how to democratically handle the non-democratic movements that keep growing stronger. Working with news, I learnt that everyone has their own reasons to influence us. I believe in the good power of each person. If we are given all sources, we form nuanced and sound opinions. That is exactly what society needs. I want to support democracy, it gives everyone the same value and responsibility.

I started working at twelve, then had my first company and was a dad at 20. Being a leader came naturally, but the rest was luck. However, I have noticed that the more we learn and practice, the more luck we have. What I do know is that we need to see beyond everyday life, believe in people, in their intentions and ability to change. I know that I need to work hard and invest heavily to gain revenue. I do not shy from conflict, or from focusing on the people that understand my vision. I always look out for new tech and think about how it can be used. If you are an innovator, tech development is good for you, since it opens up gaps to do things differently.

When we opened Fotografiska in the early days of smartphones, only a few had them. Still, we created our experience around a smartphone app and gave the young techy audience a new kind of experience. That pulled the rest of the crowd, who eventually equipped themselves as well.

Today, data and AI are about to revolutionize art—it no longer needs to be static. Pieces of art can reflect society and the observer, change with time, with what we learn and let the viewer be participatory in co-creating it. By collecting data from the environment and reflecting it back, showing all the perceptions through a specific lens of immense beauty. I would like to exhibit a living piece of art that exposes our well-being, our moods, in a gigantic immersive installation that keeps changing with the viewers.

There is a democratization that occurs when meaningful art becomes more accessible. It is then no longer stuck in one place and curated to fit historical references. Instead the art you immerse yourself in guides you into a vision of the future. Even more interesting is how we can continue the conversation after the experience, exploring how art can build relationships and an ongoing conversation. Allow works of art to become life companions, teachers, and guides. We want to drive change instead of waiting for it. If you try to be everyone's cup of tea you will be boring. And being boring is the antithesis of being meaningful.

So much of the information today is just superficial judging of distorted truths. They polarize us into silence. We need places that give credibility to the moments of insights that are born in the meeting with art. Platforms for something bigger than the everyday life outside. That anchors these experiences into hands-on contexts, enables conversations to get started and spread. That allows real learning to take place from a deep place within ourselves.

If I can contribute to that, I know my life has had a purpose. I can then be an instrument for meaningful insights and conversations that actually shape the future. That is a quest I am happy to live and die for.

—

Jan Broman *is an Entrepreneur. Creative. Founder of Fotografiska, Picture this, Fotomässan and Paradox Stockholm.*

Markus Lehto

Chasing Utopia, Finding Home

All my life I have been in one struggle or another with my environment. It's a place where my inner desires and the world's demands always seem to collide.

Nurture in Nature

The environment I was born into was near Sudbury, in Northern Ontario, Canada. It is a key part of the circumpolar Boreal Forest—better known as the *Taiga*—that covers much of Canada, Russia, and Scandinavia. It sits on the edge of the Great Lakes, the world's largest fresh water reserves, and boasts a unique range of flora and fauna that have adapted to the cold, northern climate that swings between -30 and +30 centigrade throughout the year. I recently learned that it forms the Earth's second largest biome, and plays a vital role in maintaining the balance of life for us all. Ironically, however, it is most famous for being nickel capital of the world—a result of it being the second largest impact crater on Earth, hit by a comet some 2 billion years ago. That event unleashed a bounty of minerals from the planet that continue to be mined to this day.

All in all, it is a powerful wilderness. But, it is a pretty unforgiving place to call home. It takes a certain hardiness to flourish in that environment, something Finnish people call *Sisu*—a rough blend of resilience, grit, perseverance, and an almost maniacal drive to press on despite the odds. It is a special kind of mental toughness that my parents, both Finnish, carried in their genes and expressed by the way they lived, even in Canada.

They built a hobby farm to set up our family back in the early 1970s. My dad was a teacher by day and worked on our shelter relentlessly before and after school. It was all hand made, with the support of many talented friends, most of whom were also Finnish. Within our tightly knit community were all the skills and trades, the dreams and energies, that were required to create strong buildings and lifelong relationships. There was an exchange of constant giving and receiving that helped everyone take root in a new land, free from the post-war dramas of the old world.

I really don't know how they did it. There were no architects, blueprints, or YouTube videos showing how. The *Farmer's Almanac* and *Popular Science* were the only how-to guides I remember in our home. People just knew how to do things. Even though there were some 'specialists' around, like electricians and well drillers, everyone was a jack of all trades. Those who knew more taught those who knew less, and the overall standard of competence in our community increased as a result. This form of *distributed leadership* is still the most authentic that I have ever come across.

It took a full day to walk around our property. To my child mind, it was a completely magical world filled with as much danger as beauty. We had our own lakes and swamps with beaver lodges, hills, and fields that were the threshold to the endless forest. As we climbed to the highest point on our land to look out over the wilderness—to what my dad called that 'no man's land'. He warned me about the bears, wolves, moose, deer, and wild animals that were ever presently lurking in that uncharted territory. It wasn't the animals so much that scared me, but the sheer expanse of 'nothingness', of untouched nature, that still gives me goosebumps.

Within the relative safety of our so-called 'civilized' patch, my parents raised cows, chickens, pigs, and cultivated a garden that supplied us with most of our essentials. Nature offered everything for free to those willing to do the work. There was no choice but to be biodynamic in response. That was the currency people used to make things happen. Everyone in the community shared and scratched each others backs when needed. It was *reciprocal maintenance* in action, authentically *circular* and *regenerative* by default. Life was simply like that. Necessity was the mother of invention. No one called it innovative. No one called it special. It just was. Throughout my time growing up, I sensed that we were all equal and on the same page, no matter where we were from. No one was superior by default or legacy. We were simply whole, figuring out how to do life together.

When friends came over to help on the weekends, just as soon as the tools were put away the musical instruments came out. Those who were not playing the tune were dancing or drinking to it, and often both at the same time. Around the age of 4, I picked up my dad's accordion and soon became the resident entertainer. Over the years I built up a repertoire of hundreds of songs from many cultures for all occasions. Even though I didn't really know what they all were about or really stood for, playing them held great power. Somehow, everyone knew all the words. And they evoked so much emotion that I liked playing them just to see what would happen. I was most interested in the tears, which often erupted by complete surprise. Most came from sadness and loss. My music had a way of liberating whatever surpressed emotions were there. Its purpose was to create the circumstances for the natural expression of what was inside. It created an environment.

As I reflect on those memories, though, I realize that sitting behind my accordion enabled me to distance myself from the audience. This often tempted to manipulate the 'dancers' quite a bit. I could call people to action by choosing the song and the tempo. I could make them sweat, laugh, or cry, and determine when it was all over. Sometimes I would punish my mom by playing a super long polka when she was dancing with a clumsy footed sweaty guy that had too much to drink. It was so empowering to be the observer and creator at the same time, like an analogue video game.

Now at 50 years old, I see what a gift these early moments were. I experienced a version of the world with no artificial hierarchy at any level. It was a sincere experience of *interbeing* that transcended generational gaps, species, thought silos, occupations, ethnicities and cultures. I am truly grateful for embodying those experiences the way I did. I felt like I had an important role as a pioneer, in building our own society, applying my own unique skills and talents, even though I was only a kid.

From Nowhere to Now Here

To me it feels like we've become far too civilized—probably even hypnotized—in our way of being. As we now approach the *singularity* much sooner than expected, I think there is great value in remembering what reality felt like without omnipresent screens, 24/7 media culture, and broken down neo-liberal capitalism.

A truth that sticks out for me is that close connection is essential for us to distinguish what is true and false, what is actually common sense. Many people have forgotten the importance of this, and most people of this generation are not as self-aligned and connected to nature and life as we used to be. We now live in a deep illusion, and it is getting harder to see beyond it.

It is the unique imprint of my generation, Generation X to remember its unknown quantity, *the X,* the unique state of humanity that many of us from that era experienced. I believe that people who grew up in that era hold a golden key to reigniting human spirit, having embodied the before and after of the current world system that has fully taken us over.

Thinking back to the mid 1980s, I clearly remember when multiple television channels, computers, and globalization entered our lives. Within just a few short years, the dynamics of life changed, our attention was hijacked, and we were all seduced by the thrill of the man-made world. But, is it really better?

In my family, it didn't take long before packaged food and powerful advertising replaced my mom's homemade bread and hand knit woolen socks. Going to town to buy Nike's and video games seemed much more satisfying than going into the forest to 'make wood' with my dad. It was also easier for my mom, and somehow more exciting for us kids, to buy ready fried chicken from a colorful paper bucket instead of eating our feathered friends.

Around the same time the building works in our community stopped. Everyone settled into long term mortgages and bought vacation homes. Essentials were outsourced. Entertaining at home became more and more programmed. People talked about the good ol' days but didn't live them anymore. The center of gravity switched to what was on TV—or the 'idiot box' as my dad used to call it. Now I know why: Every click of the channel came at the cost of good conversation and meaningful connection. We stopped making our own culture and consumed another one instead. We ushered in a new fake world with open arms and hollow smiles.

Being and Becoming

When I left Canada at 20, I decided to leave my accordion behind as well. While I surely didn't have enough room to lug it around with me across the world, I now think I dropped it because it was actually forced on me, like I was telling someone else's story through it. I resented it.

From the moment I showed any interest in it—and for 15 years after—I was *not-so-gently* encouraged to practice several hours a day. I studied with Iona Reed, who had become the first female accordion World Champion back in 1962. When I was around 10, my father bought the accordion that was awarded to her as the winner's prize. I was just barely old enough to lift it and get my chin over the keyboard. And surely I had no idea what the word *'virtuoso'* really meant, which was delicately—but boldly— written on the front of it in fancy looking diamonds.

I clearly wasn't ready. But, the important thing was that my dad thought it was a perfect fit. He was so excited and proud and sure I would quickly grow into it. Physically I did. But, the growing pains were largely emotional and emerged over time. As I entertained people at countless concerts, competitions, festivals, and parties, the Top 40 was playing a very different tune. None of the songs I actually liked those days sounded good on the accordion, which made it quite alienating for me to be spending so much time with it. This taught me a lot about delayed gratification and patience, to say the least.

But it also gave me powerful lessons that have universal appeal as well. One that resonates with me now is that, if you can do something 10 times perfectly back to back—and start again from 0 when you make a mistake—you will burn the process into your muscle memory, possibly forever. My teacher applied this technique on me religiously for 15 years. She was patient, but unrelenting, knowing full well that her system worked flawlessly. She said it is what made her world champion—learning things correctly 'by heart' so as to *become* them. I still make the same mistakes I made then, and have never forgotten the songs I perfected. This simple (but not easy) method of self-perfection is something we can all apply to all kinds of mistakes in our life. My life has also shown me that, if and when we don't fix them correctly, we become our mistakes. And unlearning is way harder than learning.

If I dig a bit deeper into my vault of learnings, I could also say that the accordion is actually a magical box that organizes the laws of music in such a way that you must enter into them with your full *being*. You breathe life into the music through the bellows, which demands both stamina and great delicacy. Both left and right hands—thus both sides of the brain—are fully engaged with one another, doing different things in dynamic balance. Holding the whole thing in your lap and strapping it to your body demands physical connection, strength, and nuance. There is a lot going on that you need to keep together. If you can add emotion to the mix, *harmonic resonance* is the result. You can become one with the instrument and align yourself to express the emotional vibration that stirs within you. When done right, you can experience what it feels like to *be* music, not just a musician. Sharing this with others creates *sympathetic resonance*—a sacred place of shared vibration. As its master, you *become* the creator and commander of a complex integrated system that can shape the way people move in the world. The trick is that it only lasts for as long as you can play the song, as long as you can stimulate the *anima* and *animus* of creation in yourself. The motivation to

keep it up can only come from the desire to serve others, which
I believe is ultimately rooted in the thrill of witnessing emotion
in action. This takes quite a bit of maturity and growing up to
understand.

Chasing Utopia

Though I still love creating music, I never considered the
possibility of making it my work life. The only thing that
I had ever truly mastered, I abandoned, pursuing my ideal
environment. As I contemplate this paradox, the words of my
mom have been coming to mind. When I complained about
practicing so much, she would always say "music will always
be your friend, even when you don't have any." And when that
didn't work, she went on to say, "if everything else fails, you will
always be able to make money with your accordion, somewhere,
somehow." Even the possibility of either of those two outcomes
scared me to the bone, quite like the horror I felt looking at the
endless wilderness with my dad. It felt horribly lonely.

In response or retaliation, I studied law and international relations
and had big plans to be something like James Bond. I wanted
to eat the world. I wanted to change the circumstances around
me, and I did. Yet, somehow everything meaningful I have ever
done has ended up coming back to shaping environments for
other people instead. As a real estate developer for 25 years, my
whole work life has centered around organizing the way people
come together at different scales and in different ways. I suppose
at its core, this has been my music in action—the application of
what I learned by heart in a different field, the octaves of creation
expressed in different ways.

Whether in the form of urban scale masterplans, mixed use
buildings, shopping malls, and living areas and in many countries
that touch millions of people every year, I have integrated a clear

connection and a sense of community into every development, as my inner-child sensed it could be. Interestingly, I've done this in nearly 20 countries, but never in my own 'homeland'.

Over the last decade, I've turned more deeply inward and my outward focus shifted to inverting my work life to my 'life work'. This lead to the creation of Joint Idea, Life Works Labs, and Love Mafia, an eco-system of collaboration, transformation, togetherness, and a community of communities that spans the globe. It has revolutionized all aspects of the *how* I live my life, including my relationships, partnerships, and what my work actually is.

Yet, my *why* has not changed. My focus is on community through common unity. My never ending dream is to bring all that I have learned together into a re-*creative* village, probably to continue the unfinished work of my childhood applied for our new era of possibilities. 5 years ago, tired of the classic CEO, partner, founder, and other business titles, I even started calling myself a 'Utopian' to help describe myself and what I do. It was an instinctive move that somehow came naturally—a title that I could grow into over time that reflected my actual goals, many of which I now realize are likely to take more than my lifetime to finish.

Getting the timing right has been a major challenge for me. It seems I'm always living too far in the future. Or, indeed, somewhere in the past of my memories. My music teacher actually used to scold me all the time for playing too quickly. She accused me of having a 'fire under my seat' and constantly wondered where I was rushing to. I am still in that *wonder*.

I am the Environment

To be completely open and honest, the Utopian title has been a difficult burden to bear and a nearly impossible standard to uphold. It now reminds me of the silent horror I felt when I finally learned what the word 'virtuoso' on my accordion actually meant. I wasn't ready for that responsibility as a child, but I took on the burden anyway.

This contemplation has made me think deeply about the connection between Virtuoso and Utopian, the two titles that I took into my life. I just turned to Chat GPT for its perspective. Here is what it came up with...

"The thematic connection between the two could be the pursuit of an ideal or perfection. While a 'virtuoso' represents the pinnacle of *individual* skill and excellence in a particular craft, a 'utopian' idea or vision represents an idealized, perfect state of *society* or *existence*. Both terms embody a strive towards the highest possible standards, whether in personal skill (virtuoso) or societal organization (utopian)."

After a little more dialogue it warned me: "It's important to note that while virtuosity can be realistically achieved and observed in individuals, utopian concepts are often considered theoretical, impractical, or unattainable, given the complexities and inherent imperfections of human society..."

I think this answer is just what I needed to be reminded of. It is precisely this issue of connecting the *me* to the *we,* myself to society, that has underpinned my unease with my environment in all its forms throughout my life. It takes me to a conversation with Chief Oren Lyons I had a few years ago. It turns out that the lands that I grew up in were once part of their territories, of which he is the spiritual leader. He transmitted this wisdom to me, like a reminder from Spirit: *The environment is not over here. The environment is not over there. YOU are the environment.*

I am now quite sure these powerful words hold the truth I've been looking for. The only thing I can ultimately control is my attitude, my attention, and the cultivation of my own inner environment. Whatever I do is simply an expression of that and a tool. I cannot escape from myself, no matter where I go.

What I have experienced in my various pursuits in life is the power of *common unity*; the power of our hearts and minds becoming one individually and at scale. It is the inner coherence we cultivate that ripples out to become *super*-coherence around us. Everything around us is saying the same thing, if we only had the attention to truly hear.

Epigenetics now shows that our DNA is always listening and responding, constantly manifesting our inner environment in response to our attitudes and sensory perceptions of the outside world. Physics also points out that everything is vibration, frequency, and energy. The universe is musical.

I suppose the real work of my life journey is to make it more harmonious and musical, from the inside out, to create the circumstances for emotion to flow.

And perhaps this is the ultimate contribution of Generation X— to remind the world that we are the sum average of the 5 people we spend most time with—those special ones we choose that we are most physically and emotionally entangled with. In Africa they say it takes a village to raise a child, which is so true for this reason. I am thankful to have experienced that same truth in Canada. Who are the 5 people in your life? Who are the 15 that make up your tribe? Who are the 45 that could become your village? Who are the 150 that could be become your society? How can we co-elevate each other to co-write the soundtrack of our lives? We need *real* diversity and *real* unity to grow personally and collectively. There is enormous power and social information— our living data—that transfers between us in rich cultural exchange and real community.

I learned a few months ago that the conscious human brain can only handle 16-20 bits of information per second, while the body and unconscious mind take upwards of 4 million. This shows we have higher octaves of intelligence that transcend the dimension of words, numbers, and images that we process through our conscious brains. The conscious part of our brain is not really that powerful at all. And as we are learning again and again, it is the part of us that is most easily hijacked.

My motivation for this sharing is for us to self-remember who we are as the screen based world takes up even more of our limited remaining time and attention. And as we praise the miracle of connecting to each other remotely, we must also know that it provides us far less biological information than we actually need for our daily social charge. We are all suffering from unprecedented loneliness and separation. Binary connection keeps us locked in our intellect and in the realms of the 3D world, where we experience only a fraction of the whole. We are multidimensional beings that need biological data connection and quality of presence, perhaps even more than we need food.

I hope there are some lessons to draw from this contemplation. If the television quickly changed my generation, it is easy to see how *Artificial General Intelligence* (AGI) is the biggest threat and opportunity for our immediate future. If we let screens and algorithms hijack our attention and lull us into a world of ever more comfort and convenience, we will surely wither before we know why we are here. *But,* if we recognize that novel technologies offer us the chance to exercise our responsibility to awaken our higher intelligences—that there is something more to discover about our humanity—then we do have a golden chance to create circumstances and environments that are pro-biotic and re-creative.

Put another way, virtual screen based worlds are not a substitute for the real experience of life. When we turn them off, the *real* world—the only meaningful reality—emerges. *That* is the environment that requires our immediate attention.

From this perspective, realizing that YOU are the environment is to recognize that Spirit speaks through biological structures, emotions, and relationships—not through technology, however sophisticated it may become. Only life itself can give us the information we need to duplicate and thrive. Nothing can offer us this other than the natural world. Nature is the only thing that can support real life.

—

Markus Lehto *is a Utopianist, multidisciplinary creator, community builder, and Co-Founder of Joint Idea, Life Works Labs, Love Mafia, Urbanista, and CommonUnity*

Geetali Chhatwal Jonsson

The **Storyteller**

Indian classical music has an octave of 22 notes, or 'Shruti' as they are called. My name, Geetali, means the one who loves music and it is no coincidence that it's the number of notes that can explain my journey in life so far. It has been 22 years since I moved to Sweden, built a family, career and beautiful bonds. An integrated life between India and Sweden. I travel often to India to be with my family and for work. But, it was on a trip after 22 years that I *truly* returned. I returned with old new eyes, with a new vision, a new appreciation of all that I knew before I left for Sweden and all that I have learnt since then.

This journey of contributing to the book has made me humble. We all have eyes, but sometimes we lack vision, or 'drishti'. Drishti is a balanced and focussed gaze often used in Yoga. For me it's the art of taking a moment to observe things in their totality—not to focus on one point but look at all aspects through the physical movement of the eyes. Just look away, just look up, down and beyond, there is so much more to see.

Every being is on a fulfillment journey and there is no difference in what they want from what I want. They are navigating life to bring about a positive change in their existence. It is only the methods and circumstances that are different. My narrative is not unique—all I can do is reflect upon and share what I believe is the truth at this moment.

It is interesting how we can look upon the truth differently depending on the perspective we look at it from. I remember when I was 8, my mother and I visited relatives in Delhi. We lived in the unspoiled eastern state of Assam that was quite remote at that time. On the taxi trip from the railway station I remember smelling the petrol and diesel fumes from the vehicles on the road. I associated this smell with development, excitement, new opportunities and the smell of 'success'. Today, 42 years later, I know that very smell to be polluting and undesirable. I was not wrong in my associations then and I am not wrong in my associations today. The smell is the same, I am the same, it's just that the truth the smell represents has changed.

The stories we tell often have a deeper meaning than we realise. The tradition of the storyteller has been a way to pass on lessons of life and insights that we have gathered. The stories during the centuries are essentially the same but we keep changing the context. In our family we grew up hearing stories, sharing knowledge and constantly interacting with interesting people. What has brought additional flavour to my stories is the fact that we moved around every 2-3 years due to my fathers position in the Indian Army. We were brought up curious and open minded to things that were different. Different was interesting, something new to learn. It could be the simplest thing on how to catch fish in a monsoon stream without any tools, to what crops did well in which soil. Meal times were lively and generous where all generations of family and friends gathered. This was the fertile ground where I heard my stories and made up my own. Old stories got a new form through me and I became the story-teller of the family.

I know all my stories, I have narrated them multiple times. But, each time the story comes to a new life depending on who I narrate it to. It is like the bard who sings at a moment in time to those who listen. It is an interaction between the singer and his audience that is sealed in that moment forever. To borrow a parallel from the world of music, using the words of my Forum friend Markus Lehto:

*"The most wonderful piece of music was never recorded—
it was just played and experienced by the people who happened
to be there. There is an intensely powerful beauty in that.
Something raw, fascinating, experimental that you could not
duplicate while under the pressure to record it... A spontaneous flow."*

And that is exactly how I feel about *not* writing down my stories, but simply letting them live in me and through me. They are a part of my heritage that I will pass on. I do not need to write them. I have told them all my life and they will live on in some form or another for yet another generation to discover and pass on.

Yet, as I write I dig deeper into the multiple layers that form me. Dig deeper past the layers my rational mind has created, deeper into the emotional me. The deeper I go the more I feel this sense of emptiness. An emptiness that is not empty, it is more like a portal to myself. When I come closer to the feelings of my heart and stop listening to the mind, I am surrounded by a sense of freedom. And freedom is not empty.

I am drawn to the mystics who find their truth beyond the limits of religion, society and rituals. Irrespective of the era in which they existed they all share an insight into the ultimate truth: A truth we all seek and define according to our circumstances—peace, love or whatever else we may call it. It is the truth that would take away all suffering and, yet, it is our search for the truth that causes the most suffering.

I find peace in the abstract, in the *meta*. I believe that there is something beyond what we see, feel and experience. The energies of the meta resonate and vibrate with ours, it's just that we are unaware. Our being unaware does not mean that these energies do not exist. The truth has always been there, it is here and it will continue to exist—it is indestructible. We just need friends, companions, guidance and *Drishti* to tap into it. It is just waiting for us to be found.

I feel blessed that I am in a space of faith and knowing that all of us are on the same path and will arrive at our destinations sooner or later.

—

Geetali Chhatwal Jonsson *is CEO and co-founder of home textile brand Chhatwal & Jonsson.*

Pia Rudengren

The **Silver Tapestry**

Self-esteem is to constantly embrace your inner child with tenderness and respect. There is a sacred contour to existence, a kind of conversation or correspondence with our cosmic origin, which no one has the right to interrupt, mock or sully.—Bruno K Öijer

I am looking up at the dark night sky with stars scattered all over it. They look like diamonds on black velvet. Some are small and the light is faint and some are bigger and brighter. My father is lying beside me. He explains that the small, faint stars are very, very far away. Even the big, bright stars which are closer are very far away. He tells me about star constellations and the solar system. I am in awe. He explains that we are very small compared to the universe which is enormous, even infinite. I find the concept of infinity hard to grasp and ponder it for a while.

But then he says something which bewilders me. He says that everyone, every human being, is going to die. I am only five years old and my understanding of the world around me is shattered. I know from the depth of my soul that my father is wrong. I know that I am immortal. I know that my father is immortal and that everyone I know and love is immortal. But how can my father who knows so much, whom I admire so much, be wrong about something so fundamental? This is the beginning of my lifelong search for the truth about our existence. The beginning of my pilgrim journey.

I grew up in an academic, middle class family in Sweden. Every night my father would read bedtime stories to my younger sister and me. It was the highlight of the day. He dramatized the stories and made the characters come alive from the pages of the books. We explored the world of Astrid Lindgren. My favorite was The Brothers Lionheart. I was also fascinated by *The Hobbit* by J. R. R. Tolkien and *The Chronicles of Narni*a by C. S. Lewis. All of these books are set in a fantasy world of myths and magic.

Besides my interest in fairytales and myths, I early on became involved in the traditional Swedish Lutheran Church. Where I grew up the natural gathering point was the small village church. As a teenager I deepened my spiritual quest and at the age of fourteen I decided to be confirmed in the church. I went to summer camp where the clergyman introduced us to a form of deep prayer.

The voices of monks singing medieval songs were echoing against the high vaults of the old church. We were seated in chairs with a distance between us. Silent and with our eyes closed. Thus, we could concentrate and go deep into ourselves in the meditation. The music in the background was Gregorian chants, an unaccompanied sacred song in Latin which is common in the Roman Catholic Church. A sacred feeling was evoked in me. A spark that lit my interest in the deeper and more mystical aspects of religion.

In my late teens I broadened my view. I studied Hinduism and Buddhism. At about the same time I read the best-selling book, *The Dancing Wu Li Masters* by Gary Zukav. In the book the link between modern physics, quantum phenomena in particular, and ancient eastern religions is explored. The insight that eastern religious traditions contain ancient truths only recently explored and understood by modern science, reinforced my view that spiritual truths are essential to understand ourselves and the world around us. The sense of a mystical sacred core at the heart of the universe which has always been present inside me was strengthened.

As a young adult I turned 180 degrees away from the mystical aspects of life. I fully engaged in the world outside. I chose to study business and economics at the Stockholm School of Economics and pursued a career in finance. I became the CFO of Investor AB, the publicly listed holding company of the Wallenberg group, and I later became a non-executive board member of larger and smaller corporations in Sweden and Finland.

Becoming a non-executive board member was a stroke of luck. I gained freedom and a larger sense of control over my life. With three small children I was able to dedicate enough time to them at the same time as I could explore yoga, meditation and pranayama (breathwork). These practices became a way for me to reconnect with my soul. I replaced the fairytales of my childhood with books about mystical teachings of all religions, from Sufism to Kabbalah, The *I Ching* and Theosophy. Today I have a daily practice of pranayama and meditation. Contemplation and prayer are also ways for me to reach deeper layers of truth inside me.

I started out with a strong belief in our eternal souls which led me to Christianity. After many years of explorations of mystical teachings and practices from all over the world I have come full circle, but with a higher vantage point. I can see that there are truths in all wisdom teachings and I believe that at the core all religions overlap. In the end I realize that my home is in Christianity. There is a vibration of love and grace at the core of the Christian teachings that resonates with my heart.

On Christmas Day, early in the morning, I go to a service in an old stone church in Åre, a village in the mountains in northern Sweden. The church was built in the 12th century and is located on the ancient pilgrim trail, S:t Olavsleden, which stretches from the Baltic Sea to the Nidaros Cathedral in Trondheim in Norway. During the Middle Ages this was one of the most important pilgrim trails of the Christian world, in parity with the pilgrim trails to Jerusalem, Rome and Santiago de Compostela.

The night sky is pitch black and the temperature is -24 C°. The snow sparkles from the dim light of the stars above. Outside the church there are torches that light the way. Inside it is warm and candles are lit in sconces on the walls and in the old chandeliers in the ceiling. The church is small and intimate. I take a seat in one of the old, narrow wooden benches. I listen to the old Christmas hymns being played on the organ and I am transcended to a place of deep serenity and peace. I think of all the generations before me who have gathered in the church on Christmas Day. How hard their lives were and that the only time of the week to escape the chores of daily life was on Sundays in these church benches.

I sink down into deep contemplation. I see with my inner eye a huge tapestry, a fabric made of tiny silver threads, which is holding the whole universe. The silver threads make the tapestry gleam and glisten. The fabric pervades everything. Every one of us is included in the silver fabric and we are connected through it.

I can see that everything around me; the church benches, chandeliers, the birch trees outside the windows and even my own body, contain these glistening silver threads. The silver threads vibrate and they contain the essence of life. Every breath we take, every thought, every feeling and every action we take makes the silver threads vibrate at a specific frequency and creates a wave in the tapestry. I can see the silvery tapestry ripple with the waves. It looks like a huge black sea illuminated by the silver light of the full moon.

The waves have different frequencies. When they meet they create a wave interference. Some of them cancel each other out. Some of them, if they are in phase and of the same frequency, will reinforce each other and create a wave with higher amplitude.

In our daily lives, on a micro level, we perceive the waves as impressions of our senses. They are subtle energies which correspond with the cells in our bodies. We react to them on a subconscious level. Everything we think and do will create waves which are transmitted to other people through the fabric. We are all connected and everyone influences the whole.

I zoom out to a higher vantage point where I can see the tapestry at a distance, on a macro level. There I see the reinforcing waves converge into a larger wave. Small streams accumulate into larger and larger streams until they form a mighty river at the center of the universe. The river consists of all the tiny silver threads that vibrate together in harmony.

Zooming out even further above the tapestry, the only thing I see is the mighty silver river. Everything else recedes from view. I follow the river with my gaze and I can see that it leads to a large vortex in the center of the tapestry.

I sink even further down into meditation to a place deep down inside me where my mind is quiet and where I am totally present. I tune my inner vibration in total harmony with the vibration of the silver river at the core of the universe. I feel myself getting sucked into the vortex and end up in a quiet and empty void. I hear a faint sound of silver bells chiming and I can feel a pulse coming out of the void. The realization strikes me that the void is a heart which is pulsating vibrations out into the universe. The heart is sending out love and compassion into the world.

We live in a world created by the collective mind and collective vibrations. Everyone contributes to the world we see around us. If we act out of self-interest, lacking compassion and integrity, we will create disharmony. The silver threads create waves which are out of sync with each other and the sea becomes rough and stormy. It does not matter if we masquerade as ambassadors of goodwill, and even commit acts of mercy, all we create is ripples of disharmony in the large tapestry. These waves will find other disharmonious waves, with an opposite wave pattern, and cancel each other out on the macro level. However, on the micro level where our lives take place these ripples create a lot of suffering and pain. When we proclaim that we want to eliminate suffering in the world but at the bottom of our hearts act out of self-interest or indifference, all we manage to achieve is more suffering. The reason is that the disharmonious waves create their own opposite waves in order to be eliminated on a macro level.

Everything that we think and do that creates a vibration which is not in harmony with the pulse of the heart of the universe will find a vibration with an opposite wave pattern somewhere in the tapestry. These two waves will in the end cancel each other out. Those actions and thoughts are in this sense utterly without meaning and substance. Only that which is in harmony with the pulse of the heart at the center of the universe is real.

To make a lasting difference we need to tune our own individual vibration to the pulse of the universe. We cannot change what other people think or do, but we can change inside. We must become aware of and take full responsibility for the vibrations we are transmitting. Our feelings, thoughts and actions. Every single breath counts.

Bring out your inner tuning fork. Still yourself in a quiet room. Close your eyes. Sit in stillness until you perceive the black, quiet void in the middle of the vortex which lies in the middle of your own heart. That is the point which unites us and where we can tune ourselves to create harmony. When we tune our own hearts to that pulse we will create ripples in the silver fabric which will be propagated into bigger and bigger waves of harmony.

The vibrations of the silver threads produce tones. All the silver tones aggregated create a song. When we are disconnected we create cacophony. That is how the world on a micro level is perceived today. At a higher vantage point, however, the disharmonies disappear and a beautiful song of silver tones emerges. A song filled with love. The song can be joyful or sad. It does not matter. As long as the song is in tune with the heart of the universe it is pure and true and part of the silver river. It is the song of the universe.

I am awakened from my light slumber by the organ. The pinnacle of the Christmas Day service—O Holy Night. A male opera singer makes a sublime performance of the song. My whole body starts to vibrate with the music and I believe I can hear the silvery voices of angels on top of the human voice.

—

I leave the church still vibrating with the music inside me. Outside the night is dark and the stars shine brightly, but I can detect a sliver of light on the horizon in the east. The first flush of morning. The stars in the sky are bowing in front of me. Bowing to humanity for our endless strive for a better life. Bowing to the little child inside us. Bowing to our acts of tenderness and love in the middle of chaos and darkness. Bowing to the sliver of light inside our hearts.

—

Pia Rudengren *is a Non-executive Board Member and Former CFO of Investor AB.*

Raya Bidshahri

Cosmic **Perspectives**

It was a special night in rural Iran, the stars shining brightly above. I was about four years old and remember asking my mother about the twinkling lights in the sky. I'll never forget her answer.

"They're like other suns," she explained. Her response opened a world of possibilities for me. I started imagining other worlds near those stars, maybe with little girls like me, pondering the same question.

This early encounter with the night sky sparked a deep curiosity about the universe. Growing up, I found myself buried in astronomy books, captivated by photos of stars, planets, and galaxies. I poured over photos from the Hubble telescope, in awe of the vibrant nebulas, distant galaxies, and sparkling star clusters, each one a reminder of the mysteries beyond our world.

I learned that when we look at the stars, we are looking back in time. The vast distances between us and these celestial bodies mean that their light takes years, sometimes centuries, to travel across the universe and reach our eyes. Therefore, the starlight we observe today is a relic of the past. I also learned that there are more stars in the universe than there are grains of sand on all the beaches of our planet. More specifically, astronomers estimate there exist roughly 10,000 stars for each grain of sand on Earth.

My interest in astronomy was more than just scientific; it was deeply existential. I was drawn to the cosmic perspective, a viewpoint that transcends our everyday concerns and connects us to the vast, mysterious universe.

Years later, as an education entrepreneur pioneering whole-human development, I think back to Howard Gardner's theory of multiple intelligences. Gardner, a renowned psychologist, challenged the traditional notion of intelligence being a single, general ability. Instead, he proposed a model where human intelligence is divided into distinct modalities. This theory, first introduced in his 1983 book *Frames of Mind: The Theory of Multiple Intelligences*, identifies several types of intelligence, including linguistic, logical-mathematical, spatial, bodily-kinesthetic, musical, interpersonal, intrapersonal, and naturalistic. Later, he suggested the possibility of an 'existential' intelligence, which is the ability to ponder deep questions about human existence—the way of life, the universe, and everything in it.

My passion for astronomy came from a place of this existential intelligence. It wasn't just about learning the science behind stars and planets; it was a more philosophical quest. It involved grappling with questions that have perplexed our species since the dawn of time: Why does the universe exist? Where did we come from? What is the meaning of life? These questions went beyond mere scientific inquiry, touching the realms of philosophy and spirituality.

This philosophical journey through the cosmos naturally aligns with what astronauts experience as the 'Overview Effect'—a shift in perspective that occurs when viewing Earth from space. From this vantage point, astronauts have reported a deep understanding of the interconnectedness of all life and a renewed sense of responsibility for taking care of the environment. This experience often leads to a profound sense of awe and appreciation for the planet.

You don't need to go to space to experience the Overview Effect. The perspective is encapsulated in the famous image of the *Pale Blue Dot*, a historic photo taken on February 14, 1990, as Voyager 1 was leaving our Heliosphere, more than 6 billion kilometers from Earth. At the suggestion of astronomer Carl Sagan, the spacecraft was commanded to turn its camera around and take one last photograph of Earth before continuing its long journey outwards.

In this photograph, Earth appears as a speck, less than a pixel in size, suspended in a sunbeam. This image, when coupled with Carl Sagan's eloquent monologue, powerfully articulates our place in the universe. Sagan's words, "Look again at that dot. That's here. That's home. That's us..." invite a moment of reflection on our planet's fragility and isolation in the vast expanse of space.

The Overview Effect offers a humbling yet empowering realization: while we may seem insignificant in the grand scale of the cosmos, we are, in fact, precious and possibly unique in this vast and beautiful universe. Carl Sagan, in his reflective monologue on the *Pale Blue Dot*, poignantly addresses this, saying, "There is perhaps no better demonstration of the folly of human conceits than this distant image of our tiny world. To me, it underscores our responsibility to deal more kindly with one another, and to preserve and cherish the pale blue dot, the only home we've ever known."

The *Pale Blue Dot* photo serves as a stark reminder of our interconnectedness and the shared destiny of humanity. It underscores the pettiness of human conflicts and the absurdity of claims to greatness based on geography, race, or religion. Sagan's words remind us that in the vast, indifferent expanse of the universe, our planet is a rare haven of life. He reflects on the 'rivers of blood' spilled by conquerors, all for a fraction of this dot, highlighting the fragility and preciousness of our world and its inhabitants.

This realization that no help will come from elsewhere to save us from ourselves underscores the importance of our actions and choices. It reminds us that we are not just integral but precious components of the cosmos, with a profound responsibility to cherish and protect our tiny home in the universe. This is where the cosmic perspective can be a source of human responsibility.

For me, the cosmic perspective has also been a source of spirituality, grounded not in the supernatural but in science and reality. It's a spirituality that comes from understanding our place in the universe and recognizing the interconnectedness of all things. For instance, consider the scientific fact that we are all made of stardust. This idea, deeply rooted in astrophysics, tells us that the elements constituting our bodies were formed in the fiery cores of ancient stars. These elements were scattered across the universe when these stars exploded, eventually coalescing to form planets, including Earth, and everything on it. This astounding fact connects us intrinsically to the cosmos, illustrating that we are not merely inhabitants of the universe, but we are the universe in a human form. Consider the idea that our pursuit of knowledge and understanding is more than just a human endeavor; it is the universe exploring itself through us. Our curiosity, our exploration, and our quest for knowledge and connection are the ways through which the universe experiences and comprehends itself.

This perspective has given me a sense of peace and a framework to approach the existential questions that have intrigued me since that starry night in Iran. The cosmic perspective has not only fueled my passion for astronomy but has also provided a unique lens through which I view life, humanity, and our place in the universe. It's the lens through which I set my life's mission in empowering the next generation to create an exciting future for themselves, humanity, and the planet. It's the lens through which I set my life's goals.

When I consider our education system through this cosmic lens, it becomes clear that a shift is needed: moving away from traditional schooling methods that are focused on preparing for standardized exams, towards a more intentional system of human development that makes our existence in this universe worthwhile. This human development system should aim to cultivate the overview effect and existential intelligence in the next generation. It's why our curriculum at *School of Humanity* encompasses literacies such as flourishing, thought, discovery, creativity, and more.

Embracing a cosmic perspective in education is not just about understanding the universe; it's about adopting a long-term view of our existence and our place within the cosmos. Consider this analogy to explore the vastness of Earth's history about human existence: imagine stretching your arms wide open, each arm representing the timeline of Earth's history from its formation to the present day. This timeline spans about 4.5 billion years, a period so immense it's hard to comprehend.

Now, if we were to represent the entirety of modern human history on this scale, it would occupy merely a sliver of the nail on one of your fingers. This analogy puts into perspective how recent our species is in the grand scheme of things and how brief our stint has been on this ancient planet. It's a humbling thought that underscores the fleeting nature of our existence against the backdrop of Earth's vast geological epochs.

Taking this cosmic perspective—that our existence and history are but fleeting moments in the Earth's vast timeline – is crucial for human progress. It serves as a reminder that progress, much like the evolution of our planet, can take time. Just as Earth has transformed over billions of years, human advancement too is a gradual process, marked by incremental changes and significant breakthroughs over centuries.

This cosmic perspective of space and time encourages patience and perseverance in our pursuit of human progress. By teaching our youth to see beyond the immediate, to understand the gradual march of time as exemplified by the universe itself, we can instill a sense of responsibility for the future and a deeper appreciation for the slow yet impactful progression of human advancement.

—

Raya Bidshahri *is the Founder and CEO at School of Humanity.*

Ma Steinsvik

Stories of Wisdom

On the ragged shore of snowclad mountains, a growing wind tears the hems of a small, stern woman. Her gaze is fixed upon a small boat out on the open sea. In it, young children desperately lift heavy oars again and again. The Maelstrom has no mercy with those who sneak out of a safe basin to fish the richness of its tomb. Inch by inch it pulls the boat towards the grim gulf of the ocean, the arctic night already coloring the horizon with sorrow. The mother knows, now is the time for praying. Ancient words flow over her lips, silent but harsh like the pebbles under her shoes. Wrestling with the rising voice of the wind, contesting the unforgiving forces of the life she has chosen. Not a twitch, not a sound leaves her lips as the boat painstakingly slowly starts to turn.

She does not hug her children as they pull the boat up onto the shore. She brings them home to the warm soup waiting on the stove. People later spoke about a golden cord that seemed to drag the boat back, the boat they all thought was doomed. But not one was surprised; everyone knew the power of her faith.

A lifetime later, at the terrace of a metropolitan penthouse, my grandfather would still yearn for the taste of that soup and the prayers to which he owed his life. He honored her magic and built something she would have been proud of. A global house of stories, an international web of people dedicated to those stories that have the power to transform us. He left us early but made sure I was aware of the golden cord we both carried inside before he went.

I was sometimes embarrassed to tell friends I could not meet up because my father was reading to us. But not listening to him was unthinkable. As his voice flew through the pages, we experienced how primordial dragons coloured an ancient sky, awed at the green beauty of the Uruguayan pampas and felt the heat of the desert from a flying carpet. We befriended the brave people of all complexions that inhabited these adventures from around the world. As we traveled with them, they taught us how to live.

In the enchanting games of the Scandinavian Sagas, trolls and elves instilled that it is up to us, and only us, to write the stories of our own lives. A young princess left the castle to seek her brother in the deepest forest. When she was but a small sick girl, he had struck a deal with death and sacrificed his shadow in return for her health. But without his shadow, people felt uncomfortable around him. He was forced to leave the country to never come back. Finally old enough to search for him, our princess embarked into the deep forest at the northern borders. She encountered three grim trolls, who demanded her beauty, youth and health in return for a ball of golden yarn that directed her to the prince. Now an old woman, she found her brother who recognized her as she gazed into his eyes. The power of love restored her youth and they returned to rule the country that was theirs to inherit. We instantly knew that we too must take on the responsibility to be courageous and helpful. To accept our shadows and never give up.

But the lessons were not only about ourselves. In another tale, a cruel snake-king ruled the country and demanded a new wife each evening, who was then found dead in the morning. When the turn had come to a gentle baker's daughter, she used her wits instead of succumbing to her fears. She tricked him into peeling off the layers of his skin in a barrel of water. As she cleaned off his seventh layer, the bewitched prince inside could be freed. They ruled together side by side for as long as they both lived. Her patience and courage freed him. Because she knew that every human being has a golden cord inside all our layers.

As seasons passed, these stories were our companions. The gifts of generations; deep insights lie encoded within them. They are the DNA of our civilization. Without them, we are lost. They instill in us the truth that wit, grit and pure hearts are rewarded in the end. When we learn to cherish nature and all life, listen to the softest of voices, trust the weakest of signs, treasure our imagination, we are freed to blossom into our true self.

Those are the treasures of Sagas and tales, crafted collectively to guide the future. Literature on the other hand is the work of individuals. To me, writers are heroes. They create playgrounds where their characters try out choices and directions, with the imagination of the reader as participant. I got to enter this magical world early. The welcoming library of our house was filled with gems. My mother's precision made sure a book would emerge just when I could begin to grasp it. After dinner had been cleared away, we would scrutinize the main characters' every action over a steaming hot chocolate.

In my mother's safe presence, I could formulate the unbearable lethargy of Mme Bovary, the heartbreaking honesty of Kristin Laurensdottir and the absurdity of Candide's unclouded optimism. I later realized that the library was a living planthouse, a simulator where I could learn from experiences unlived and start to understand the nuances that bridge good and bad. Most importantly, I learned that every person, no matter how complex, could be understood. That every situation can be solved. If only you pay close attention and listen.

But the gift of literature went deeper. When I turned teenager, I struggled with a world that seemed agonized by broken promises, shattered dreams, and rage of frustration. Then Plato whispered through the millennia. He invited me to the world of ideas that is hidden from us in the cave-world of illusions where we reside. Herman Hesse's Siddhārtha told me the path led through the practice of stilling the mind. It made my golden cord inside resonate with something I had always known. At night, I searched every scripture, every book of creation I could get my hands on, for clues towards that path I knew must be my own. In my external life I continued to deliver, completed an MBA, worked abroad to then make my family's house of stories and the emerging tech my mission. But something was wearing me down. I did not understand then, that in our lives, everything must be one. That our inner life must be aligned with the manifestation of our actions. That the voice calling us towards our purpose, must be the master of our choices.

Years later, the lamps above me were fluorescent and cut through my pulsing forehead. Paper sheet on a padded stretcher scratched sore skin, as I tried to find out where I was. A nurse gently cleaned blood from my hair, and from a deep cut that deformed my brow. I had fainted from work and the second child I had carried no longer lived inside me. The look on my little son's face as his father came to pick me up, made me promise to halt and change. I had been so absorbed by leading, by completing endless tasks, that I had forgotten to ask myself why. When my own pillow granted me sleep that night, I somehow knew that stories would again come to my rescue. They had told me that we all have a path of our own, and it is our task to muster up the courage to find it. I would light up that golden cord of my great-grandmother, it would not lead me astray.

Soon after, a sign on a subway told a story of yoga. My golden cord lit up and soon yoga became a part of my daily practice. It peeled off my layers as mind-chatter gave way to exquisite stillness. It guided me towards the truth we all access from within. I started teaching yoga in my spare time, combining the new knowledge with the stories of old. I have found that often in life, a radical shift is not the solution. It is having the courage to take the first step and the endurance never to stop walking. As I took the step towards a daily inner practice, I embarked on a path towards my purpose. Outside my window, singing cranes of the Arctic pass as they cross the continents. They too follow an inner calling that lights up like a cord inside them, until they reach the home of their dreams.

Gradually, my worklife transformed. Still within the framework I was born into, life and graceful friends brought amazing possibilities into my life. Inspiring people and projects came my way. Most of all, I felt at peace. I woke up to gratitude and realized my emotions did not influence me the way they once had. Instead, my focus and intuition grew strong. A new precision entered life. I could read people, truly listen and understand signals of transformation in the world. I did not have to give up leading companies or being a mother, just be more of the one I have inside me. And I had discovered the joy of sharing.

I now know that all leaders need contemplative practice to accompany their journey and am grateful every time I may help. I found my purpose; to guide global change leaders towards transformation. With them, I create meditations, stories of their lives, with archetypes that guide them onwards. Finally, the different parts of my life are united. The work with companies, my inner journey and the guiding all complement each other. That golden cord I inherited has woven my life together, a seamless tapestry of all the nuances of life.

So why do we need an inner practice? Let's listen to the stories. In the Bhagavad Gita, Prince Arjuna is called to war, but does not want to fight the well-known faces that are lined up in the army before him. His armor and sword are too heavy to bear. But his mentor, Lord Krishna, explains his duty. To rid himself of fears and move against the dark forces. He must save his country. This is how it feels to conquer one's own darkness. We all have it. Shadows and a darkness inhabited by fearful emotions. Stored away in the deep corners of our body. Hidden, because these emotions were just too fierce and painful for the children we once were. Trapped as they are, the emotions grow forceful over time and start influencing our decisions and actions. Like dragons they awaken and steer us astray. In the Lord of the Rings, Gollum was engulfed by the precious possession he could not let go of. Just like him, in stressed situations we live out unsolved dramas and repeat what once caused the pain. We judge the present and fight with people around us. Instead, like Prince Arjuna, we can use our clarity and solve the situation for the good of all. And now is the time to do that, there will never be a better moment than this one.

When we are led astray by our own demons, we lack the sense of meaning that Viktor Frankl taught us is necessary to live fully, yes even to survive. In his masterpiece 'Man's search for Meaning' he explains how at scale, we otherwise collectively create a world that reflects the darkness inside of us. But, we have a choice, we can rise to the occasion. Integrity flows like a wellspring inside you. It strengthens every time you choose to follow it. A contemplative practice will silence the chatter in your head enough for you to hear its voice. It is not an easy path, but like Prince Arjuna, or any of our childhood heroes, we may choose to face the challenge.

One breath is all it takes to enter the chamber of our body. From there, we can observe the wave of emotion as it passes through and over us. Every time we choose to sit with our emotions instead of acting them out, pain diminishes. Until one day we can surf upon the waves, become dragon riders.

I now know why as a teenager I felt that the world was bent. When we try to live without the old stories, without contemplative practice, it is like jumping through life on one foot, refusing to use the other foot that is our birthright. We become slow, frustrated and off-center. The external shift to a regenerative system must be accomplished through an internal shift. As Gandhi said, peace starts within. In an ever more challenging and complex world, we need to know how to move into inner stillness. There, we have the integrity to adhere to the value of all life, to the awe-inspiring heaven that is our earth. The heaven that we are born into. No matter what the external world demands, we will choose what we know is right. This in turn will inspire others. We might not know exactly where the road is heading, but the golden cord will make sure we find our way home to that warm soup waiting on the stove. Where we are at peace.

—

Ma Steinsvik *is CEO of Bulls Holding, Board Executive, Investor & Advisor. Principal, Business Leader, Keynote Speaker, Board R&B Licensing, Gutsy Animations.*

Raj Sisodia

The Human Journey

We are given life, but we must choose how we are to live.

How we live determines how we and others will feel when we leave this life. Will we feel a sense of satisfaction, with no regrets and surrounded by loved ones? Will others feel GRIEF? Or will they feel RELIEF?

The answer depends on whether we can heal our wounds and traumas and live a fully human and intensely loving life. That means consistently striving to act consciously rather than compulsively; cultivating our personal power; discovering and living our purpose; and always acting from love.

To me, the human journey distilled down to its essence is this: we start out as unconscious and powerless; our journey through this lifetime is to become conscious and empowered—awakening to what really matters and being an instrument of that which seeks to emerge into the world.

A Brief Shining Moment

Most of us go through life oblivious of the reality that our lives are incredibly short, and could end any minute. On November 12, 2020, my friend Danny Friedland received a diagnosis of terminal brain cancer. Danny told me that when he stepped through the door to the doctor's office, he thought he had abundant time remaining in his life; on the other side, he learned he had a very finite amount. It turned out to be less than 12 months.

The night after I learned about Danny's diagnosis, I had a clear vision in a dream: "You're dying. Now live like it." Life is a terminal condition for all of us. The message was clear: use every day, every hour, every minute mindfully, to have a positive impact on others and leave a legacy of love and healing.

Most of us sleepwalk through our lives in a kind of trance. We must awaken from that trance and make the most of this precious gift of life.

Like most of us, Danny had deluded himself into believing that he had "infinite time" remaining in his life. An average newborn in the US has about 26,900 days to experience life. At my stage of life, I probably have about 6900 days remaining. It could be as many as 9000—or as few as one. That is a scary but bracing realization.

We all have a very finite amount of time – infinitesimal on a planetary scale. Many people in the world have extraordinary amounts of money and power, but all of us have limited time, notwithstanding the desperate efforts of many billionaires to cure the "disease of death." I shudder to think what would happen if they succeeded. That which we recognize as scarce becomes precious. As Steve Jobs said in the face of his own imminent demise, "Death is very likely the single best invention of life."

However limited, our time here carries within it infinite potential for creating beauty, spreading love and enabling transformation. It is incredible what humans can do in a day, even what we can do in just 90 minutes. It took Viktor Frankl nine days to write *Man's Search for Meaning*—a book that has impacted hundreds of millions of people and is considered by the Library of Congress one of the ten most important books ever written.

It's one thing to awaken; it's another thing to *stay* awake. Speaking from a place of absolute clarity as he faced the end, Danny said, "Stay awake to what really matters: the intense giving and receiving of love."

In the precious days he had remaining, Danny channeled precious, loving wisdom on behalf of all of us. Overflowing with love and urgency, Danny told me, "Swimming in these waters is delicious. I've never been this content and happy. I don't think that would have happened if I had a less dire diagnosis."

Think about that: Danny was grateful for his terminal diagnosis.

Be a Healer and an Artist

So how should we use the limited time we have been given? I believe each of us should strive to become healers and artists, regardless of the work we do.

Why do we need to be healers? The answer is simple. We live in a world that has an extraordinary amount of unnecessary suffering.

Most of this suffering is caused by human beings towards other human beings and other life forms—especially factory-farmed animals, tens of billions of which are killed every year after living tortured lives to satisfy our ravenous appetites. The only conscious, loving response to suffering is healing, which I define as alleviating suffering, elevating joy and enabling healthy growth. All life is precious. We share this planet with millions of species, each of which is designed to live its life in a particular way. Every lifeform finds its deepest fulfillment when it fully lives into the blueprint of what it is uniquely designed to do.

Human beings are unique in one very important way. All other beings are programmed to live out their lives in a predetermined way; we humans are the only ones who can self-author our lives. We are endowed with extraordinary capacities of imagination and the ability to create. That means that we can all be artists. Sadly, few of us realize this, and settle for the dull and mundane in our lives.

Picasso said, "Every child is an artist. The problem is how to remain an artist once we grow up." Sir Ken Robinson tells a story about a six-year-old girl that illustrates this. "She was at the back, drawing. The teacher… went over to her, and asked, 'What are you drawing?' The girl said, 'I'm drawing a picture of God.' The teacher said, 'But nobody knows what God looks like.' The girl replied, 'They will, in a minute.'"

What does it mean to be an artist? It is about giving full expression to the creative impulses of our souls. It is about imagining and manifesting that which does not exist. Our life is the canvas on which we can deposit the outpourings of our soul to create something of lasting value and transcendent beauty. If we do not lean into those capacities, we are not living fully human lives.

Living an artistic life is about pursuing "the good, the true, and the beautiful." Originally articulated by the Greek philosopher Plato, we now know them as the "platonic ideals." A very similar idea exists in the Indic tradition, captured in the phrase *Satyam Shivam Sundaram,* meaning "Truth-Godliness-Beauty." When ideas such as these spontaneously spring up across diverse geographies, cultures and eras, they are pointing to universal truths that we should all pay attention to.

The FILMS of Your Life

My core message to you is this: we should live every day being exuberantly and fully human. That means using all our gifts to the fullest. Unique among all the beings on this planet, humans have a sophisticated capacity for language, enabling us to connect deeply with one another and build on each other's ideas to create the incredibly sophisticated world we inhabit today.

We also have other qualities that make us unique that we do not use as much as we should: free will, imagination, the ability to laugh, a moral compass, and self-awareness (summarized as *FILMS*). These are qualities we should consciously cultivate to lead the most human lives possible.

Free Will—We have the capacity to act independently of self-imposed constraints, but most of us tragically fail to do so most of the time. We are free beings who live as though we are caged or otherwise enslaved.

A few years ago, I played a board game in which each player was allotted several 'action cards' that gave them the power to make certain things happen in the game. The game has very few rules, but most players assume that the rules that commonly apply to other games also apply here. This is a common failing of human beings: we assume rules and constraints that do not exist.

At the end of the game, when one person 'wins', it is invariably the case that each of the other players is left with a stack of unused action cards; they had held onto them in anticipation of some future situation that never arose.

Ask yourself, "What action cards am I holding that I haven't even realized?" Make sure to play them all before your life ends – which could be any moment.

Imagination—This is perhaps the most magical of human capacities. It renders us essentially divine. Unique among all living beings, we can imagine something that does not exist and bring it into existence. It could be a poem, an idea, a book, a machine, a building, a mass movement—anything at all.

Look around you. Everything that you see that is not part of nature existed inside a human mind before it appeared in the physical world. The world is as you dream it. If you don't like the world as it is, you need to dream a better dream.

For the first 40 years of my life, I believed I was "just an analytical, left-brained engineer incapable of creativity." Once I shed that limiting belief, I entered the most productive and impactful phase of my life, resulting in ground-breaking work that transformed my life and laid the foundations for the Conscious Capitalism movement.

Ask yourself: "How can I free my imagination? What can I create that doesn't exist but needs to? What is the more beautiful reality that is possible?"

Laughter—Some animals cry with pain and hunger. But humans alone have been granted the gift of laughter. Why is that? Just as we can consciously use our breathing to shift our emotional state, we can use laughter to impact our state of being. Laughter causes the brain to release chemicals that help us relax and feel good. It makes us breathe deeply, use our muscles and activates our heart and lungs. Laughter can soothe us when we're feeling worried or scared.

I have always had a good sense of humor, honed further when I became a passionate fan of the British author P. G. Wodehouse. But over time, I became much too serious in my life. I now see that I need to stay connected to my inner child, the "fool" that lurks in each of us, and recognize that life is often a theater of the absurd.

Ask yourself: "What am I taking too seriously in my life? How can I find the humor in every situation?"

Moral Compass—Human beings are self-interested creatures, but we are also hard wired with a deep need to care and a moral compass that helps us distinguish right from wrong. Too many of us have allowed our moral compass to become warped or dysfunctional. We need to repair and sharpen our moral compasses.

In his short story "The Death of Ivan Ilyich," Leo Tolstoy wrote "What if all the things the most highly placed people said were the right thing to do were false, and my scarcely perceptible impulses, which I immediately suppressed, were true?" The deeper I got into my business education, the further I receded from my sense of right and wrong. I was taught that everything was about making as much money as possible while staying within the letter of the law. I eventually recognized the folly of this and started to question the ethical implications of every action and decision. That too was instrumental in creating the Conscious Capitalism movement.

Ask yourself: "How can I act in harmony with my deepest sense of what is right and just?"

Self-Awareness—As Walt Whitman said, "I contain multitudes." Plumbing the depths of our psyche is a lifelong adventure. It is a journey that we should be on until we draw our last breath. Understanding ourselves (and others) is one of the most important tasks assigned to us humans.

For the past two decades, and especially for the last five years, I have been on a journey of getting to know myself, love myself and be myself. Every time I think I have arrived at clarity about myself, I soon realize that there is another level to explore. Ask yourself, "Who am I? What makes me unique among all the people who have ever lived? How can I fully manifest my gifts to bring what is missing into that world?"

—

You are the author of the screenplay of your life. What do you want the narrative arc of your life to be? What kind of a film would it be? Is it a tragedy? An epic? A feel-good story? A story of nihilism? One of hedonism and self-indulgence? Is the movie of your life distinctive or formulaic? Is it uplifting, inspiring, life changing? Is it a story of redemption or a cautionary tale for what not to do?

Let me return to the question I started with. How will others feel when we leave this life? Will they feel GRIEF? Or will they feel RELIEF?

My father was a brilliant, powerful man, but he was not rooted in love. When he died, there was very little grief, only a sense of relief. My mother was an incredibly loving, caring soul, but she never claimed her personal power. When she died four months after my father, there was an immense outpouring of grief. The lesson to me was clear: we must live in a way that at the end of our life, people experience deep grief, mingled with deep gratitude for the life we had lived and the lives we had touched. This comes by cultivating our personal power while being rooted in love.

Remember, we are given this incredible gift of a human life, but it is up to us to make something of lasting significance with this gift. Let us resolve to live a fully human, joyful, and artistic life in service of the good, the true and the beautiful.

—

Raj Sisodia *is an author, a FEMSA Distinguished University Professor of Conscious Enterprise and Chairman of Conscious Enterprise Center at TECNOLOGICO DE MONTERREY.*

Rebecka Carlsson

The Speaker's Journey

I want to devote this little text to something I believe is incredibly important: *That we should be empowered to proactively create narratives for the world we're dreaming of.* And perhaps more now than ever.

Recently, I published the book; *The Speaker's Journey—7 Steps to Create the Important Narratives & Speeches for Our Transformative Times.* I'd like to share what I've found to be true through that writing process. When I read the other essays in this book, I noticed how they stayed with me, and greatly shaped how I viewed the world in the weeks that followed. I could find myself in a meeting, suddenly being more interested in the *Silver Tapestry*, just to name one example. This reminded me—once again—of the worlds and opportunities that open when others are generous enough to share their inner worlds with us. And that this might be the crack where the light gets in, for us to follow out of this permacrisis and Silent Spring, to what can hopefully become a better next life chapter and a Loud Summer.

So, I'd like to dedicate this manifesto to you, my friends in the Corporate Unplugged Forum, and to all of you who decide to share your knowledge, wisdom and dreams, so they can be of value to many more of us. Thank you in advance!

Transformations – Narratives – Speech

We're entering exceptionally transformative times. And if we are to restore the Garden of Eden and create a paradise on Earth, we have narratives to create. Great narratives for the world we want to see, and smaller ones for more specific knowledge and wisdom. We also say this all the time: "We need new stories for the future." But let's actually create them. It's also important that we spread them to the world. Speech is the most human, and therefore powerful form, of communication we have. And in the times we're in, we'll need the most human and powerful forms we've got—though we should be empowered to use other creative forms too.

Imagination & Speech

Humans have two superpowers: *imagination* and *speech*. And through speech, imagination can become *a common*—think of a common grazing land; a shared resource for all. Communication means just that; "*to make common, share or impart*" originating from the Latin word *Communicare*. So, through speech we can take what we see in our imagination and make it into a common, so that we can then jointly act upon this now shared dream.

Speeches are Portals

Speeches are portals. Almost magical. With them we can bend

time. Because it's fully possible to walk into a room and *think, know, feel and do* in one way, listen to a speech for perhaps thirty minutes, and then walk out and *think, know, feel and do* in a way you would never have done otherwise. The question becomes: *Who do you want to take from where to where, and how?*

The Right Speech

If we are to create a *definition* of a good speech, it shouldn't be about the speaker, and not even about the speech, but about the *function* the speech will have in the long run: What effect it will enable. What it does for us. What it actually gives. A good speech is very close to what, in Buddhist practice, is seen as *the Right Speech*. There is, of course, a deep well of meaning to this definition, but summarized it's about communicating what is both *true* and *helpful*. So, 'a good speech' is essentially the 'Right Speech', and 'a good speaker' is anyone who gives the 'Right Speech'.

The Hero's Journey

The Speaker's Journey refers to—as you might have concluded already—The Hero's Journey. In the mid 1900s, Joseph Campbell mapped out this structure that so many stories follow in *The Hero With a Thousand Faces*, and his several other now classical works. He found that most stories and myths follow this same structure—and portray the same archetypes —despite originating from vastly different places, traditions and times. And drew the conclusion that this *Monomyth* is essentially *stories of human transformation*; and not only a pattern for most external transformations, but really *a pattern of the human psyche*. And not only a pattern for *individual human's transformations*, but also for *humanity's transformations as a whole*.

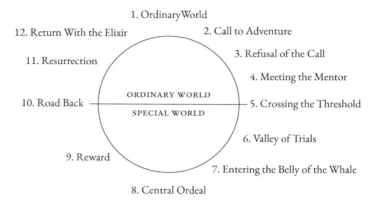

The Speaker's Journey

So then, where does speech play a role in *The Hero's Journey* and human transformations? In several parts: the Call to Adventure, the Meeting with the Mentor, in the Central Ordeal and Resurrection, and in the Return with the Elixir. A speech can hence both be the *final* step of the Hero's Journey—which makes the journey worth it—as well as the *first* step and the Call to Adventure for someone else. Bees have a particularly sophisticated way of communicating when collecting pollen for honey. All bees will fly out on individual hunts and explorations in all kinds of directions. In a way they're flying on their own daily Hero's Journeys. When a bee finds pollen it will return to the beehive and do a little dance by which it communicates where the pollen is, so that all bees can fly there and enjoy it. To not give your speech when you have one that would benefit others, is to find the pollen but not bother to do the little dance because of, for example, being too self conscious of looking stupid or silly. To not give a speech when you have one to give is to *not* deliver someone else's Call to Adventure, *not* be someone's Mentor, refuse your own Valley of Trials, Central Ordeal or Resurrection, and to *not* share your Elixir upon your return. A good speech *not* given is therefore essentially a missed opportunity for humanity and a more perfect union on Earth.

The Leader's Journey

The Speaker's Journey is also The Leader's Journey. Because in a way, leadership can be reduced to, *telling the right story, to the right people, at the right time.* By doing so, the group will be able to see reality clearly, as well as their place in it, and how they can act. It is actions that change the world; but words that change our actions.

Humanity's Hero's Journeys

So, Hero's Journeys happen for humans, for collectives, and for humanity as a whole. As collectives we are also regularly called to adventures, might refuse these calls, meet our mentors, and finally, hopefully, decide to transform into more evolved versions of ourselves. When creating narratives with the intent to support such greater transformations, we can work through the following three steps: *1. Transformation:* What's sacred or the most important to us? Therefore, what transformations are we called to? *2. Narrative*: What narratives would help us realize it? *3. Speech*: How can the narratives best be spread to the world?

Transformative Narratives

We are now entering exceptionally transformative times where any attempt to list all transformations standing before us quickly reveals itself to be naively inadequate. We cannot comprehend the magnitude nor all aspects of what awaits us. But, we do know we're called to several Hero's Journeys:

Ecological—essentially about reintegrating humanity back into the ecosystem.

Societal—essentially about developing better ways of collaborating for the opportunities and challenges of our time.

Spiritual—essentially about redefining what it means to be human.

We also know that we'll need transformations, and therefore new and better narratives, at all levels of society:

Human—as the narratives we tell about ourselves.

Group—as the narratives we tell about our family and friends.

Organization—as the narratives we tell about, for example, our company.

Community—as the narratives we tell about, for example, our city or village.

Nation—as the narratives we tell about our country.

Region—as the narratives we tell about our continent.

World—as the narratives we tell about our humanity, earth, and universe.

In these transformative narratives we're, in essence, reformulating the answers to these ten questions:

'Who are we?'
'Where do we come from?'
'Where are we at now?'
'Where are we heading if we continue as now?'
'Where do we want to go, and who do we want to become

instead?'
'What's sacred or the most important to us?'
'Therefore, what's the problem?'
'What's the solution?'
'If visualized, how would the world be with it?'
'What's our call to action?'

Generative Stories

Creating narratives often requires a lot of work. Just because they're immaterial doesn't mean they're easy. Hopefully one day we'll become as sophisticated in developing our narratives as we are in developing technologies. When we eventually get the stories right, they become 'generative'—thus sometimes called *Generative Stories or Generative Narratives*—and the organization or movement seems to start moving almost by itself because everyone just knows how to lead themselves within the whole in the right direction. Perhaps, creating narratives will be one of our most important works for the coming decades? We have placed a great deal of focus on developing technologies. But, without the meaning-making component, these structures and processes seem hollow and, at worst, destructive. So, we will likely want to focus a lot more on the narratives and other immaterial aspects in the decades ahead.

Speaking Starts With Listening

An important principle in this work is that, 'speaking starts with listening'. Because it is through listening to the world, and into ourselves—to what we hear, and what we don't hear—that we will be able to hear what stories want to be told, and which stories are our stories to tell. Only from this listening can we speak in a way that is truly creative and capable of adding our unique value to the world.

Spiritual Practice & Collaborative Act

At best, and over time, creating narratives and speeches becomes a deeply personal and spiritual practice—like a great spiral—through which we circle deeper and deeper into ourselves and what we wish for the world. This spreads further and further out into the world and into direct contact with more and more people.

Let us come together and create narratives and speeches as a collaborative act. In times of crisis it's easy to end up in despair and loneliness. But what have people done in all times of crisis throughout history? They've come together in a circle and talked about it. So, now is a good time to convene—to listen to the world, each other, and ourselves—and talk about what's sacred and most important to us. What transformations are we called to? What narratives would help us realize them? How do we best spread them to the world?

—

Rebecka Carlsson *is a sustainability entrepreneur and author, former political advisor to Sweden's Minister for Climate and the Environment, and partner at ARC.*

After **Words**

The Lotus

The Lotus reminds us that all life is born from the mud of the Earth and nourished by the past, and strives upward through a fluid world, eventually opening radiantly into space and light.

Throughout history, the Lotus has captivated humanity's imagination and search for deeper meaning. Ancient Egyptians revered the flower's daily cycle of opening and closing as a symbol of the Sun's perpetual rebirth. In Hinduism and Buddhism it represents purity, enlightenment, and the blossoming of our Chakras—the energy centers within our subtle bodies that bridge the physical and spiritual realms.

The Lotus rises in a magnificent display of elemental harmony. Its roots delve deep into the earth's embrace, while its stem gracefully pierces the water's surface. The wind carries its sweet fragrance, and the sun's warmth awakens its ethereal bloom. This transcendent flower embodies the Spirit and interconnectedness of all things and also mirrors our own human experience. We, too, are 'mud born' creatures. Yet, within us lies the potential to be creators, to rise above life's challenges and blossom in the light of truth.

Our personal essays intertwine, like the petals of the Lotus, exploring the realms of the earthly and the ethereal in a quest for our *Rays of Truth*. By choosing the Lotus as our symbol, we self-remember that we can always rise above opposing forces, transcend the limitations of duality, and tap into higher realms— the spaces within our higher selves. This is where we encounter Truth in its purest form: a knowing that comes not from the mind, but from direct experience.

The Power of Process

The thing that matters most in life are not made of matter at all. The feeling of connection and wholeness can only emanate from our heart, when trust and love emerge from genuine experiences of unity. This cannot be bought, faked, traded, or artificially produced.

As a community of individuals that have all achieved success in their own respective fields, we in the Corporate Unplugged Forum discovered that this feeling, Love—the Mother of *all* connection—also needs a 'project' to come to life.

Rays of Truth became that project. Creating it was an adventure revealing how our personal stories combined, which gave us new perspectives into ourselves, each other, and the world we live in. This is something we rarely, if ever, get the chance to manifest in our busy everyday lives.

Over 100 days of contemplation, self-reflection, and a very different kind of writing, our words revealed their blossoms. Without a clear plan, without an agenda, without a publishing contract, without a paid professional team, we entered the unknown, opened our hearts, rolled up our sleeves and said "let's do this!" and figured it out as we went along. It became love in action.

Though it was also hard 'work', the act of writing, compiling, editing, and formatting our truths was as much a gift to ourselves as it hopefully is to you, dear reader. It led to unexpected insights and new paths for our personal and collective growth. We found that the unifying question at the heart of the book fostered a profound sense of authenticity and courage. It revealed new things about ourselves and our community, making us stronger and more cohesive, and showed us there are powerful ways for us to work and produce in joy that are not typically possible. We felt synergies that showed us we are more than the sum of our parts, far more together than alone.

We consciously chose the personal essay format as a way to honor the approach of renaissance philosopher *Michel de Montaigne*. Today, we are all going through our own rebirth, as individuals and society as a whole. At a time when artificial intelligence and emerging technologies both dazzle and terrify us, the personal essay format taps into something deep within that helps discern the real from the fake, the true from the false. It is a powerful way of making sense of the world. At a time when we are shifting from a model of capital scarcity to *attention* scarcity, this may be the most important human skill we need to develop our conscience and reclaim deeper meaning in our lives.

Our process revealed to us the unique challenges and gifts of writing and reading something that comes from deep within. It was a healing journey that helped us remember why we are ultimately here on this Earth at this critical point in time.

From the very founding of the Corporate Unplugged Forum, we have called ourselves the *Dreamers who Do* with the *Courage to Care*. Creating this book showed us that there are also next levels on the journey, starting here with our *Courage to Share*.

—

Dear reader, revealing and sharing your Rays of Truth is a practice we encourage you to seriously consider. It is a deep and impactful process that generates trust, connection, and love that can strengthen the heart of your own body, your circle, your community, your organization, and humanity as a whole. If what you have read in these pages resonates with you, we invite you to reach out and explore how our experiences and ongoing inquiries in the Corporate Unplugged Forum can serve your organisational and societal mission.

Scan the QR code to connect and access
the Corporate Unplugged Forum, the
Corporate Unplugged Podcast, and other
content for *Rays of Truth*

Reflecting on My Rays of Truth

Reflecting on My Rays of Truth

Reflecting on My Rays of Truth

Reflecting on My Rays of Truth

Reflecting on My Rays of Truth

Reflecting on My Rays of Truth

Printed in France by Amazon
Brétigny-sur-Orge, FR